JOSEPH

“The Prophet Joseph Smith.” Godwin.

JOSEPH

AN EPIC

ZACHARY McLEOD HUTCHINS

All illustrations in *Joseph* have been provided by Godwin, an artist who looks to the work of Albrecht Dürer, Gustave Doré, William Blake, Francisco de Holanda, James Tissot, Hans Baldung, Franklin Booth, and Jacob Boehme for inspiration. His art, which is collected at the Library of Godwin, links The Church of Jesus Christ of Latter-day Saints and Mormon folklore to centuries of Christian art through classical archetypes and the symbolic grammar of mysticism.

Manufactured in the United States of America
1 2 3 4 5 C P 5 4 3 2 1
∞ This book is printed on acid-free paper.

Cataloging-in-Publication Data available
from the Library of Congress

ISBN 9780252046902 (cloth : alk.)
ISBN 9780252089022 (paper : alk.)
ISBN 9780252048463 (ebook)

for my father
in heaven

CONTENTS

PREFACE

From his first declarations of heavenly visitations and gold plates, Joseph Smith became a symbol of American exceptionalism. The global religious movement he birthed is grounded in an account of Jesus Christ visiting and healing and teaching ancient inhabitants of the Americas shortly after his resurrection, and because the record of this extrabiblical gospel was engraved on gold plates buried near Joseph's boyhood home in Palmyra, New York, his recovery, translation, and publication of the record provided a divine origin story for the United States and a prophetic vision of the nation's future. Further, Joseph framed his own prophetic calling in the context of a heaven-ordained national commitment to pluralism and religious freedom. North America, he taught, would be a gathering place for the elect of all the earth; it housed sacred sites, including the location of Adam and Eve's biblical paradise and the place where his followers would build the New Jerusalem. As a result, the story of Joseph Smith and The Church of Jesus Christ of Latter-day Saints is ineluctably bound to providential narratives of American history.

Even those who reject his theological claims have come to regard Joseph Smith as a representative American, the self-made man whose life epitomizes a national lore of original thinking and inspired action. Reflecting on Smith's legacy, the literary and cultural critic Harold Bloom wrote that

> what matters most about Joseph Smith is how American both the man and his religion have proved to be. So self-created was he that he transcends [Ralph Waldo] Emerson and [Walt] Whitman in my imaginative response, and takes his place with the great figures of our fiction, since at moments he appears far larger than life, in the mode of a Shakespearean character. So rich and varied a personality, so vital a spark of divinity, is

> almost beyond the limits of the human, as normally we construe those limits. To one who does not believe in him, but who has studied him intensely, Smith becomes almost a mythology in himself.[1]

Even those who reject Joseph Smith's foundational claims, that he saw and conversed with God the Father and with Jesus Christ and with angels, cannot help but regard his story as a compelling case study in the American imaginary—a reminder that colonists and early citizens of the United States regarded the North American continent as a place of unparalleled opportunity, where the impossible was made manifest.

Some treatments of the prophet's life have, accordingly, leaned into the fantastical. Orson Scott Card's six-novel *Tales of Alvin Maker* sequence attempts to deal with the supernatural elements of Joseph Smith's life story by setting it in an alternate world, where magic is commonplace. Card recasts Joseph as Alvin Miller, the seventh son of a seventh son, whose magical abilities allow him to reshape the natural world. Like Joseph, Card's protagonist confronts skeptical religious leaders, including the Jonathan Edwards–inspired Reverend Philadelphia Thrower, and receives a midnight visit, in his bed, from a Shining Man who commissions him to restore all things. Card's novels are entertaining and address important moral problems, but displacing Joseph's story into a world of fantasy effectively dodges the most pressing questions raised by his account of heavenly messengers: What does it mean for angels and devils to be active participants in our own, material world? What is God's role in the affairs of nations? If God appeared to Joseph, how can we explain his apparent absence or inaction, in the face of others' suffering and supplication? Why might an impoverished and relatively ignorant adolescent like Joseph Smith be chosen as God's mouthpiece? Joseph's story is saturated with supernatural elements, but his claims must be situated in the known world, or the most challenging questions implicit in his narratives of heavenly visitation are stripped of their potency and relegated to the realm of fantasy.

Most accounts of Joseph's life adopt the opposite approach, hewing so closely to demonstrable facts and historical sources that they, also, eschew the essential questions of visions and angels and miracles. Richard Bushman's *Joseph Smith: Rough Stone Rolling*, published in 2005, is still the biographical benchmark, and he treats the prophet's life with meticulous care, grounding every claim in the voluminous primary source material documenting Joseph's life. But such sources are, necessarily, finite; not every event or exchange can be memorialized, so confining our consideration of a subject to the documentary record necessarily relegates important private matters to the dustbin of history. For example, historical sources cannot address questions about miraculous means and divine silence or recreate the intimate, undocumented moments shared between Joseph and Emma during their courtship and marriage. Such scenes and questions can only be considered through an imaginative approach that supplements the extant record with inference and analogy and conjecture to reclaim the joy, whimsy, despair, and uncertainty of Joseph's surreal life. The goal of such an approach to Joseph Smith's story is not a more minutely accurate account of his actions but a greater appreciation for the pathos of his experience and the implications of his claims. Ironically, a life substantiating the maxim that truth is stranger than fiction might only be fully appreciated by turning to a fictionalized narrative as the means of reclaiming its full wonder and strangeness.

Only the epic is capacious enough, as a genre, to capture both the historical and the supernatural sweep of Joseph's cosmological story, which situates the prophet *in medias res*, caught up in a conflict between God and Satan predating the world's creation and hastening, through Joseph's prophetic labors, to its conclusion. A genre equally committed to theomachy and national history, the epic poem presupposes the intervention of divine beings in human affairs and frames politics as an outgrowth of providence. In other words, an epic renders human experience in the same terms in which it was understood by Joseph Smith and his followers, who thought of their conversion to the restored gospel of Jesus Christ as a form of participation in the eschatological vision of Revelation: their distinctively American piety pitted against the forces of Satan in a spiritual battle preparing the way for Jesus Christ's Second Coming. To rewrite the story of Joseph Smith as an epic poem, therefore, is to restore the prophet's own imaginary, considering the implications of a literal conflict between hostile, invisible, infernal powers and the benevolent, visible, heavenly beings who taught a New York farm boy to think of himself in heroic terms.

Of course, the heroes of epic poetry—Achilles, Odysseus, Aeneas, Dante, Satan, Adam, and Clarel, among many others—are deeply flawed individuals whose fame is as much a function of their foibles as their exploits. So, too, was Joseph Smith, who willingly dictated a series of revelations documenting his own failings and has been the target of vitriol since his youth. Accordingly, this poem begins and lingers in the interrogative mood, asking whether Joseph is worthy of either the praise or the censure he has attracted over the past two centuries; neither hit-piece nor hagiography, it takes the prophet and his narrative seriously without neglecting elements of his story that might be discomfiting to those who revere him as a paragon of virtue and speaker of heavenly truths. The Joseph readers first meet here, in iambic pentameter, is an embodied teenager who spits and farts and sweats; whether those bodily functions, or sinful but altogether human inclinations to sloth and greed and lust and wrath, are compatible with the character of a prophet is a core question of the poem. That question is also representative of the larger dilemma posed by attempts to treat Joseph Smith's narrative of religious experience as history or fantasy. History can account for the healing of Joseph's leg, which was almost amputated because of a typhus infection, but it cannot corroborate Joseph's claim that Jesus Christ, in his role as the Great Physician, healed him of sin's wounds and declared him forgiven. Fantasy might paint a picture of the supernatural vistas opened to Joseph's eyes, when God the Father and Jesus Christ descended from heaven into a grove of trees, but it also forsakes any pretense to the representation of reality. The epic is, from our modern perspective, a hybrid form conjoining the visible and invisible worlds, and the epic hero is a similarly syncretic blend of otherworldly strengths and unmistakably mortal failings.

Although the epic has often been given up for dead, this poetic account of his life is a wager that what modern readers sometimes find off-putting in epic poems like *The Divine Comedy* or *The Canterbury Tales* is not their form or their content but antiquated allusions and language. Modern readers forget that when these and other epics were first declaimed orally or committed to paper, they were voiced in a vernacular accessible to all audiences and spoke to contemporary controversies as well as more timeless topics. The epic harbors encyclopedic aspirations and addresses eternal conflicts, but it is also the outgrowth of a specific historical context. Over the twenty years I have been at work on this poem, I have also been immersed in national conversations on the ethics of torture, the definition of marriage, and the future of democracy. Just as John Milton's first readers saw the English Civil War of their own, recent past as an essential subtext for his presentation of a premortal war in heaven, those who read *Joseph* will naturally recognize their own experience of American politics in the war of words and tumult of opinions Joseph Smith confronted during his adolescence. In other words, the prophet's story is presented here in the form of an epic poem because that is still the best genre for performing the dual task of situating him within the broader historic and literary tradition appropriate to his stature as the founder of a major world religion while also considering the continuing relevance of his story to our own conception and experience of divinity and national identity.

Both Joseph's contemporaries and those who have contemplated him from the distance of decades considered the epic form indispensable to a proper chronicle of his life. Bayard Taylor, whose rise to fame roughly coincided with the death of Joseph Smith in 1844, thought the martyr's story a fit subject for his *magnum opus* and published *The Prophet: A*

Tragedy, in 1874. Thirty years later Orson F. Whitney, an apostle of the Church, composed an epic that ranges from a premortal council in heaven to Joseph Smith's vision of a future day when Church members preserve the United States from downfall: "Ephraim saves / Columbia's soul from chaos."[2] Two of the more notable twentieth-century Latter-day Saint epics are R. Paul Cracroft's *A Certain Testimony* (Deseret Press, 1979) and *The Nephiad* of Michael R. Collings (The Borgo Press, 1996), both of which devote more time to the retelling of biblical and Book of Mormon accounts than to Joseph's nineteenth-century life. In short, Joseph Smith and the Church and the scriptural records surviving him have attracted epicists aplenty over the years, but these literary accounts of the prophet's life and legacy have largely been ignored by readers.

This neglect might be attributed to the decline of poetry, as a vehicle for both leisure and edification, over the course of the nineteenth and twentieth centuries. But the perpetual interest of readers in new editions of the *Iliad* and the *Odyssey* suggest that form is not an impediment if the subject is of sufficient interest, and Joseph Smith is a figure whose importance to the American mythos only seems to grow over the course of centuries; as debates over Christian nationalism and religious freedom grow more strident, his relevance to contemporary political and religious questions becomes more and more apparent. Like many of these new translations of Homer, this narrative of Joseph's life reads like prose, forsaking the archaic language and syntax that readers of Geoffrey Chaucer or Edmund Spenser might associate with English epics. Anyone who appreciates a good novel will be able to understand and enjoy the story unfolding in these pages, yet those with an ear for meter or an eye for the poetic line will appreciate that the narrative's form provides a metacommentary on the prophet's life above and beyond the explicit message of its language.

Joseph is divided into two volumes, each of which can be read independently—potentially in a single sitting. Samuel Johnson complained of *Paradise Lost*, "None ever wished it longer," and that accusation applies equally to many other epics, which prolong their narratives with asides on a wide variety of subjects.[3] However, readers should, by design, finish each of these volumes with an unsettling sense that more must be said. In his thirty-ninth year Joseph's life was cut short by an assassin's bullet, and many who study his career have expressed curiosity about what he might have accomplished if afforded additional decades. His death was a disquieting event that troubled his followers, many of whom believed that his story would end in triumph, at the Second Coming of Jesus Christ. Readers might find these volumes similarly disquieting, as the arc of his life is unexpectedly cut short in each. The first volume, *Awakenings*, ends in despair, but an informed reader will know that remarkable spiritual experiences and accomplishments are around the corner for Joseph. The second volume, *New Covenants*, ends in contentment, but again, an informed reader will know that serious controversy and adversity would arrive to afflict the prophet and his followers shortly after its concluding scene. The aim of these foreshortened narratives is to provide new vantage points from which to survey the life and legacy of Joseph Smith, seeing him not as the static martyr of 1844, robbed of possibility, but as a figure whose future is still indeterminate, unsettled. The confused and troubled boy whose anguished cry concludes volume one is a very different figure from the confident and contented father appearing at the end of volume two. Each volume tells a different story, featuring a different cast of characters; the prophet's parents, who feature prominently in the first volume, are succeeded by Emma Hale Smith and Oliver Cowdery in the second, and Joseph is himself transformed in the intervening white space.

And yet, both volumes are part of a larger whole whose structure draws attention to the multiplicity of history. Each is composed of 2,500 lines, and careful readers will recognize similarities in the language, ideas, and events presented in parallel passages. For example, in the early lines of *Awakenings*, Joseph listens to a preacher declare the necessity of entering into a baptismal covenant:

"But
admission to perfection's pastures can't
be gained by sinners half so vile as you—"

(Now Joseph saw that bony finger wagged
his way, now felt himself condemned by God)

"—unless you first incline your head, accept
his yoke, and join the fold by baptism."

In the equivalent section of *New Covenants*, Joseph asks Emma, whom he is courting, to accompany him on an errand to retrieve the golden plates from the angel Moroni, and she responds with a condition:

"Just promise that, when God
asks you to form a new society,
you will remember us—the ladies—too."

He bowed his head and promised her, "Yes."

"Thank
you," Emma answered. "That will do for now,
until Moroni comes to give the book
into your custody."

The repetition of a single word (*head*) in line 166 of each passage creates a linguistic tie between *Awakenings* and *New Covenants*, and the broader parallels in plot raise questions about ecclesiastical authority, gender, and the nature of covenants or promises. Either passage could stand on its own, but reading vertically, across volumes, renders the poem a commentary on itself, introducing new perspectives on language and events a reader might have considered closed—in the past.

Some two hundred such linguistic and thematic parallels link *Awakenings* and *New Covenants* together, and many of these address the complexities of history explicitly, through a second structural device. Both volumes embed commentary on well-known historical events in line numbers that correspond to the year in which they occurred. For instance, the first volume speaks of Joseph "discovering some brave new world of wealth" in line 1,492, a nod to the year in which Columbus arrived at Hispaniola. But the second volume provides a check on this seeming celebration of colonial greed by identifying Columbus (recognized by Church members as that "man among the Gentiles, who was separated from the seed of my brethren by the many waters") with the Book of Mormon's archetypal villain, Laman, in the corresponding passage:

> And it came
> to pass that they cast lots, and Laman thus
> was separated from his brethren by
> the Spirit of God; or, it seemed to them
> that God had given the disposing of
> the lot into his lap. But Laban thrust
> him out and said he was a robber come
> to steal the record of his brethren in
> the church and threatened to cut off his hand
> if he should come again, pretending that
> he was a beggar.

From a perspective lionizing Columbus as the herald of New World wealth to a recognition that he approved cutting off the hands of innocent Taino men and women, the poem resists conclusion by insisting upon an iterative, incremental revelation of meaning across its two volumes. *Joseph* lingers in the interrogative mood, cultivating increasingly refractory, multifaceted views of history.

Although its titular figure is never off stage for long, the poem frequently gives voice to perspectives other than Joseph's own, ranging from family members and friends like Mary Whitmer and Lucy Smith to figures from sacred history, like Mormon and Satan. *Awakenings* is divided into three books, and the first introduces a teenaged Joseph to readers, situating his questions about ecclesiastical authority within a larger family tradition of religious seeking. Book II introduces a demonic council that takes up the question of how to prevent Joseph from seeking revelation from heaven, and Book III describes an event that Church members commonly characterize as the First Vision, when God the Father and Jesus Christ appeared to the youth with a message of forgiveness and with instructions about his role in restoring to the earth a fullness of the gospel of Jesus Christ. *Awakenings* then concludes with a relation of the angel Moroni's charge to the prophet that he retrieve plates of gold from a nearby hill and translate the ancient record inscribed thereon. *New Covenants* picks up the narrative four years later, on the cusp of Joseph's trip to retrieve the plates. In Book IV, he marries Emma and, after moving to Pennsylvania with the plates to avoid persecution, makes an initial effort at translation. Book V is a reconstruction of the translation's first pages from the Book of Lehi, which Joseph dictated to Emma, recounting an alternate version of the ancient history found in the Book of Mormon. Readers are introduced to a family of refugees from Jerusalem who make their way to the Americas by boat, to establish two competing civilizations whose founders Joseph Smith identified as the primary ancestors of Native American peoples. Book VI returns to Joseph's own story, describing his efforts to publish the Book of Mormon and to organize his growing band of followers into a church in Ohio. The poem concludes, then, at approximately the halfway point of Joseph's prophetic career, at a moment when he might still have expected a future far different from the one we are familiar with in biographies and histories of his life. In this way, *Joseph* reenacts the tragedy of a life cut short, but its final lines are, paradoxically, a portrait in contentment, depicting the prophet surrounded by his family and followers in a blissful moment of rest—as he might have hoped to conclude his days.

Of course, the poem also ends with a mention of the young woman Joseph hired to help Emma care for their children and keep house: Fanny Alger, whose relationship to the prophet has been the subject of much speculation. Thus, in its ending, as in many passages throughout, the poem accepts Joseph's own account of heavenly guidance and heroic deeds as a factual baseline but incorporates other, less flattering perspectives on his behavior and motivations in an attempt to develop a fuller sense of the man. My understanding of the early history of polygamy and other controversial questions has been shaped both by a careful study of primary sources, from the records compiled by Joseph and his family and followers to the testimony and accusations of his contemporary critics, as well as a consideration of the voluminous scholarship on Smith's life and legacy. Many of the most important primary sources have now been published online in *The Joseph Smith Papers*, which include court records and personal reminiscences of Joseph's career as a treasure hunter as well as the attestations of early Church members, who affirmed that the prophet was directed by angels. Readers in search of a modern perspective on these sources may wish to consult a brief bibliography, appended to this introduction, identifying some of the most important works of scholarship I consulted during the research and writing process.

However, this bibliography makes no mention of the many literary sources with which I have been in conversation over the last twenty years. That omission is intentional, a purposive silence. Michael Chabon memorably observed that "every work of art is one half of a secret handshake, a challenge that seeks the password."[4] The pleasure of giving that password is akin to that of unexpectedly reuniting with an old friend—seeing Rebekah in the countenance of that Samaritan woman at the well, or recognizing King Lear's voice in the soliloquies of Captain Ahab—and is too great to spoil by preemptively and tediously documenting every bit of banter with the dead in which an author engages. Readers with eyes to see might notice that I tip my cap to Ralph Ellison in the poem's first verse paragraph and find some gratification in supplying the other half of the secret handshake extended in those lines. But I believe the prophet's story is propulsive in its own right and that readers disinterested in my necromantic inclinations should be able to enjoy tracking Joseph Smith's growth from adolescence to adulthood without worrying about missing an homage to Ellison or Emily Dickinson or C. S. Lewis or Friedrich Nietzsche. Rather than draw back the veil and identify all my interlocutors, I will simply note that literature is a conversation and that learning to recognize its rhythms and recurring cadences has been one of the great pleasures of my life. Those determined to give the other half of Chabon's secret handshake and pass through this veil of silence will, I hope, find in that experience a fraction of the pleasure I have enjoyed in reading the words that now stand for and in behalf of my chosen literary ancestors, as proxies that allow me to converse with them and enter into their presence.

I first conceived of this project two decades ago, before I had even met Ellison or Nietzsche, while washing my laundry by hand in Brazil, where I was serving a proselytizing mission for the Church of Jesus Christ of Latter-day Saints. As I wrung out each article of clothing, I listened to Truman G. Madsen's celebratory lectures on Joseph Smith and dreamed of retelling his story in verse. The poem, as I imagined it in Brazil, was to be an unambiguous celebration of the prophet and his divine mission. Twenty-two years later, I am still a devoutly practicing member of the Church, and I still believe that Jesus Christ revealed himself to Joseph Smith, commissioning the boy prophet to translate the Book of Mormon and to organize a church that could administer saving and exalting ordinances. But I am, today, far more aware of Joseph's flaws and foibles—the failings that he himself acknowledged in canonized revelations and casual conversations as well as those alleged by his adversaries and disaffected followers. And I feel deep compassion, today, for close friends and family members who experienced their own, belated realization of his humanity as a form of harm or betrayal. As a result, this final product is a much more nuanced expression of my faith than I could have imagined twenty years ago. It is an epic poem that equivocates, inviting readers to consider for themselves whether a beloved LDS anthem like "Praise to the Man" is still the lyric best suited to a twenty-first century understanding of his life and legacy or whether a novel hymn might better encapsulate his contributions to the cause of Christ, to the Church, and to the American mythos he embodies.

Notes

1. Harold Bloom, *The American Religion: The Emergence of the Post-Christian Nation* (New York: Simon and Schuster, 1992), 127.
2. Orson Ferguson Whitney, *Elias: An Epic of the Ages* (New York: The Knickerbocker Press, 1904), 141.
3. Samuel Johnson, "The Lives of the English Poets," in *The Works of Samuel Johnson*, volume 6 (London: 1824), 161.
4. Michael Chabon, *Manhood for Amateurs* (New York: Harper, 2009), 5.

Sources Consulted

The following compilation of scholarly work on the life of Joseph Smith is by no means an exhaustive list of the works I consulted while conducting research for this project. But it should point readers interested in the question of my sources to a representative sample of the most influential books and articles I reviewed throughout the writing process.

Adams, Dale W. "Doctor Philastus Hurlbut: Originator of Derogatory Statements About Joseph Smith, Jr." *John Whitmer Historical Association Journal* 20 (2000): 76–93.

American Apocrypha: Essays on the Book of Mormon. Edited by Dan Vogel and Brent Lee Metcalfe. Salt Lake City, UT: Signature Books, 2002.

Americanist Approaches to the Book of Mormon. Edited by Elizabeth Fenton and Jared Hickman. New York: Oxford University Press, 2019.

Anderson, Richard Lloyd. "Circumstantial Confirmation of the First Vision Through Reminiscences." *BYU Studies* 9.3 (1969): 373–404.

Anderson, Richard Lloyd. *Investigating the Book of Mormon Witnesses*. Salt Lake City, UT: Deseret Book, 1981.

Anderson, Richard Lloyd. *Joseph Smith's New England Heritage: Influences of Grandfathers Solomon Mack and Asael Smith*. 2nd edition, revised. Salt Lake City, UT: Deseret Book, 2003.

Ashurst-McGee, Mark. "Moroni: Angel or Treasure-Guardian?" *Mormon Historical Studies* 2.2 (2001): 39–75.

Bradley, Don. *The Lost 116 Pages: Reconstructing the Book of Mormon's Missing Stories*. Salt Lake City, UT: Greg Kofford Books, 2019.

Brewster, Quinn. "The Structure of the Book of Mormon: A Theory of Evolutionary Development." *Dialogue: A Journal of Mormon Thought* 29.2 (1996): 109–40.

Brodie, Fawn M. *No Man Knows My History: The Life of Joseph Smith the Mormon Prophet*. New York: Alfred A. Knopf, 1945.

Bushman, Richard Lyman. *Joseph Smith: Rough Stone Rolling*. New York: Alfred A. Knopf, 2005.

Bushman, Richard Lyman. *Joseph Smith's Gold Plates: A Cultural History*. New York: Oxford University Press, 2023.

Butler, Jon. *Awash in a Sea of Faith: Christianizing the American People*. Cambridge, MA: Harvard University Press, 1990.

The Coming Forth of the Book of Mormon: A Marvelous Work and a Wonder. Edited by Dennis L. Largey, Andrew H. Hedges, John Hilton III, and Kerry M. Hull. Salt Lake City, UT: Deseret Book, 2015.

Compton, Todd. "Fanny Alger Smith Custer: Mormonism's First Plural Wife?" *Journal of Mormon History* 22.1 (1996): 174–207.

Compton, Todd. *In Sacred Loneliness: The Plural Wives of Joseph Smith*. Salt Lake City, UT: Signature Books, 1997.

Cross, Whitney R. *The Burned-Over District: The Social and Intellectual History of Enthusiastic Religion in Western New York, 1800–1850*. Ithaca, NY: Cornell University Press, 1950.

Gardner, Brant. *The Gift and Power: Translating the Book of Mormon*. Salt Lake City, UT: Greg Kofford Books, 2011.

Givens, Terryl L. *By the Hand of Mormon: The American Scripture that Launched a New World Religion*. New York: Oxford University Press, 2002.

Givens, Terryl L., and Matthew J. Grow, *Parley P. Pratt: The Apostle Paul of Mormonism*. New York: Oxford University Press, 2011.

Hartley, William G. *Stand by My Servant Joseph: The Story of the Joseph Knight Family and the Restoration*. Salt Lake City, UT: Deseret Book, 2003.

Hill, Marvin S. "Joseph Smith and the 1826 Trial: New Evidence and New Difficulties." *BYU Studies* 12.2 (1972): 223–33.

Jessee, Dean C. "The Earliest Documented Accounts of Joseph Smith's First Vision." In *Opening the Heavens: Accounts of Divine Manifestations, 1820–1844*. Edited by John W. Welch and Erick B. Carlson. Salt Lake City, UT: Deseret Book, 2005. 1–33.

Joseph Smith: The Prophet, the Man. Edited by Susan Easton Black and Charles D. Tate. Provo, UT: Religious Studies Center, 1991.

MacKay, Michael Hubbard. "Event or Process? How 'the Chamber of Old Father Whitmer' Helps Us Understand Priesthood Restoration." *BYU Studies* 60.1 (2021): 73–104.

Madsen, Gordon A. "Joseph Smith's 1826 Trial: The Legal Setting." *BYU Studies* 30.2 (1990): 91–108.

Madsen, Truman G. *Joseph Smith the Prophet.* Salt Lake City, UT: Bookcraft, 1989.

Morris, Larry E. "Oliver Cowdery's Vermont Years and the Origins of Mormonism." *BYU Studies* 39.1 (2000): 106–29.

Morton, Sunny McClellan. "The Forgotten Daughter: Julia Murdock Smith." *Mormon Historical Studies* 3.1 (2002): 35–60.

Newell, Linda King, and Valeen Tippetts Avery. *Mormon Enigma: Emma Hale Smith.* Urbana, IL: University of Illinois Press, 1994.

Nibley, Hugh. *Lehi in the Desert; The World of the Jaredites; There Were Jaredites.* Volume 5 in *The Collected Works of Hugh Nibley.* Salt Lake City, UT: Deseret Book, 1988.

The Prophet Puzzle: Interpretive Essays on Joseph Smith. Edited by Bryan Waterman. Salt Lake City, UT: Signature Books, 1999.

Quinn, D. Michael. *Early Mormonism and the Magic World View.* 2nd edition, revised. Salt Lake City, UT: Signature Books, 1998.

Romig, Ronald E. "The Lamanite Mission." *John Whitmer Historical Association Journal* 14 (1994): 24–33.

In Sacred Loneliness: The Documents. Edited by Todd Compton. Salt Lake City, UT: Signature Books, 2022.

Taves, Ann. "Discerning Supernatural Presences: Experiential Claims and Restorationist Movements in the Burned-Over District." *John Whitmer Historical Association Journal* 40.1 (2020): 20–38.

Taves, Ann. "First Vision Controversies: Implications for Accounts of Mormon Origins." *BYU Studies* 59.2 (2020): 73–94.

Vogel, Dan. "Evolution of Early Mormon Priesthood Narratives." *John Whitmer Historical Association Journal* 34.1 (2014): 58–80.

Vogel, Dan. "Joseph Smith's Family Dynamics." *John Whitmer Historical Association Journal* 22 (2002): 51–74.

Walker, Ronald W. "Martin Harris: Mormonism's Early Convert." *Dialogue: A Journal of Mormon Thought* 19.4 (1986): 29–43.

JOSEPH

AWAKENINGS
VOLUME 1

No poems can please long, nor live, which are written by water-drinkers.

—Horace

The poet knows that he speaks adequately, then, only when he speaks somewhat wildly, or, "with the flower of the mind"; not with the intellect, used as an organ, but with the intellect released from all service and suffered to take its direction from its celestial life; or, as the ancients were wont to express themselves, not with intellect alone, but with the intellect inebriated by nectar.

—Emerson

I

Praise to the Man? That hymn to him who lives
and died in ages past reflects the faith
of those who knew him, saints who knelt with him
in prayer and pressed his palms in love. Today,
I make no claim to carnal knowledge but
with broken knees assume the posture of
petition, asking thee to grant me that
peculiar disposition of the eyes
required to re-illuminate the flesh
and bones of an invisible man's life.

Please, Father: send thy Spirit to inspire
me, as the resurrected Son consoled
his ten apostles (two were absent then:
the one who doubted and the traitor who,
for thirty silver pieces, sold his soul)
before commanding them to edify
the world with truths undimmed by human tears.
Teach me, before December dies away
and birthday celebrations cease, to see
his long-snuffed light—like Galileo, through
a glass, or like Columbus, when he looked
across the sea for signs of Cathay and
proclaimed its splendors to the Queen—that I
might learn to sing this novel hymn of praise.

Who first unfurled bright freedom's banner on
these western shores and bore winged liberty
to every nation, tongue, and people? No

author of civil war can claim that he
accomplished such a thing—not Washington
or Jefferson, not Lincoln, Johnson, or
the Bushes. Presidents make governments
and governments make war; but their wars buy
too dearly rights whose purchase cannot make
men free. For men are not made free by rights
or laws and statutes bound in time. Truth
alone can free a man from slavery
and sin, and only after he had seen
the Father and the Son could Joseph Smith
republish verities embodied in
that vision and unchain the minds of men.

Despite his youth and ignorance, the gods
endowed him in this knowledge when the boy
knelt, stripped of pride, to ask which sect taught truth
and which to join—a natural request,
considering the frenzied period
in which he adolesced. Religious zeal
arrived in nineteenth-century New York
with all the ravening celerity
observed in birds of prey descending on
a tender, tasty little lamb, to stir
the ashes of devotion's memory,
until an ember of belief, thought cold
and dead with Whitefield's passing, burst to life,
igniting and consuming souls who threw
themselves from spiritual slumber in
the fields and forests of Palmyra to
the anxious bench, a consciousness of sin,
and new concern for their salvation. But
although this rush of penitents appeared
the earnest of ecclesiastical
prosperity and peace, a bickering
of shepherds—crooks assembled slantingly
in corners, they debated whether their
burnt-over mutton had been charred by the
itinerant enthusiasms of
Methodist preachers or, perhaps, by one
too many *Plain and Serious Address*

on Family Religion, sent by the
Connecticut Society and its
Baptist equivalents—suggested that
denominational disputes would long
delay the advent of millennial
affinity in this American
pursuit of Reformation.

Preachers sparred
like pugilists. Their verbal brawling bred
new doubts, endangering adoptive claims
on Abraham, as cautious souls refused
to join, reject, or otherwise display
a preference for the different tribes, lest by
their choice they err, offending Deity.
Those willing to affirm a creed and risk
affiliation in this war of words
could only stand between the lines and wait
to feel that aural fist whose fearful blow
would drive them to their knees. Such struggles for
conversion often raged without reprieve
for weeks, extended till the Spirit and
its fruits retreated.

Late in the fall
of eighteen nineteen, Joseph entered in
the fray, expecting—even hoping—to
become a casualty of Christ. Nine times
already nightfall had pursued the light
from its assault when Joseph first caught sight
of that embattled canvas hall. The tent
was bleached with years of use but still blocked out
the sun's most brilliant rays, and though he stood
a stone's throw off, too far away to see
beneath the blackness of that sailcloth throat,
he heard its diatonic voice:

"Fear not
ye fallen sons of Eve! Cast off the gloom
of mortal woes and look for better days
ahead. Your fates have not been written yet
in God's great book of life and death; no man

has sunk so low that he, by dint of sweat
and tears and toil, cannot escape the chains
of Hell. Perfection lies within your grasp,
if only you will raise your hands and reach
for God; the Lord says 'If you *feel* for Me
then you will find My love'—Have *you* reached up
to find Christ Jesus? Reach my brothers! Stretch
my sisters! Lift your arms and *feel* his love!"

Though Joseph's limbs flew into motion at
the frenzied climax of that sermon's broad
crescendo, zeal was not the force that drove
his pumping fists and flying feet. Concern
so conquered both his filial regard
for time and sense of fear that when he heard
the keening shrieks that sounded after speech
had ceased, he ran, in hopes of helping those
poor sufferers escape the torments and
afflictions that occasioned their lament.
Proximity, however, gave him new
perspective on their pains; no sting or scourge
apparent to his view distressed the men
and women writhing there in dust. Unsure
of how to aid, young Joseph joined instead
the circled throng around some ten fallen
bodies, each more unsightly than the last.
The nearest Joseph barely recognized:
his features frozen in a grimace, limbs
spasmodic, jerking like hooked fish—a clerk
at the McBride store. Next to him lay two
more men afflicted with the malady,
whose closeness caused the couple to attack
each other every time their arms convulsed.
Hands flailing with infernal guidance fell
on noses, ears, and eyes, and sometimes slipped
down south to knock upon the abdomen
or chest. Apparently oblivious,
these boxers landed blows that thudded out
a dull percussion for the howls and moans
emitted by the members of that band,
whose voices warbled variations on
a theme of suffering.

Soon Joseph, lost
in contemplation of those three and their
companions, started from his scrutiny,
awakened as the minister renewed
his contretemps with sin: "These chosen few
have reached perfection, and their souls will find
God's rest on earth." Then, realizing that this
assertion might appear incongruous
with bodies flailing on the ground, he paused,
a solemn look upon his countenance
that matched the long black coat he wore. In tones
more thoughtful than before, the preacher gave
an explanation: "Having seen their own
unworthiness, they shrink and shriek before
the wrath of God—a painful price, yet one
that you'll agree is reasonable and
that must be paid by all of Adam's sons
who hope to taste God's milk and honey. But
admission to perfection's pastures can't
be gained by sinners half so vile as you—"

(Now Joseph saw that bony finger wagged
his way, now felt himself condemned by God)

"—unless you first incline your head, accept
his yoke, and join the fold by baptism.
Only the penitent, first justified
by water, can be sanctified with fire;
and not just any baptism will do.
The thing must be done properly, by one
who's got authority, and I performed
their baptisms myself, not more than nine
or ten short months ago," acknowledging
his groaning back-up singers with a nod
before continuing, "and whence is *my*
authority? From Thomas Coke, a man
ordained by John Wesley himself, who laid
hands on him as Moses on Joshua.
But you, sir," pointing to a careworn pair
of eyes, "what if your infant son were sick?
He *must* be baptized here lest heaven bar
its gates at death. To whom and what would you

FIGURE 1. “A Religious Fervour in the Land.” Godwin.

entrust your son's eternal welfare? To
the Reverend Beeston and his Princeton-won
diploma? Or to Elder Hartwell and
the congregation that elected him
a preacher? No, but trust in Joshua
and Moses. Trust the Bible, which provides
a pattern in all things. Trust—"

Once again
the howlers interrupted, rising up
in unison to celebrate their joint
election. Each described a vision of
the beatific scene. Unique accounts
and voices swirled together in the rush
of praise to paint a vague, impressionist
collage of "Hallelujahs," punctured by
sporadic exclamations more distinct
than those that formed the standard hue and cry.
One claimed she saw three iridescent rings
wheeling in flames around an effigy
of human shape; another said he spied
the Son astride a chariot whose wheels
and carriage sawed the air with eyes that blinked
out bolts of lightning.

Joseph listened to
the strange reports of each, and when the last
had finished, he departed with the dusk,
resolving to attend that gathering
where next the preacher would appear. He left
the still excited scene content to lose
himself in thought, though careful not to let
his feet meander with his mind; the moon
was thin, and he'd be late for supper as
it was. But seven mouths were quite enough
to keep his parents occupied, and they
postponed their questions till the night's first chill,
and gentle scolding, gathered children to
the hearth.

Assembled there, they waited for
the question that invariably marked
the close of every night: "What good have we

performed today? Don Carlos?" Three-year-old
enthusiasm filled his youngest son's
response, and Father Smith disguised his mirth
in solemn nods and twinkling eyes, then turned
to Katharine for her report.

                                        A sly
expression passed across her face, and then
she answered: "My good deed was to forgive
when William tripped me in the orchard lot."

But William, who had been expecting this,
half muttered in reply, "Just sore because
you couldn't catch me," and his parents took
the bait. As Mother scolded, Father roared,
and all the children fled like tumbleweed,
driven before the storm that Katharine
had summoned; for, unlike that Gordian noose,
whose interwoven twinings wound around
and through each other in a fibrous maze,
inseparably bound, the ties that knit
a family together and to God
are simple, easy equally to knot—
and absent daily tightening, unknot.

Mother and Father slowly gathered back
their charges to begin the ritual
again, but entropy and sin had sapped
its power. William and then Samuel
gave rote replies, so few were listening
when Senior spoke to Junior: "Son, what kept
you from returning home on time? You know
your mother worries for you when you're late.
Did some good deed detain you at the Wells'
place?"

        Joseph's hands, a man's, ran through his thatch
of golden flax and lifted up a boy's
face—troubled eyes of blue that sought relief
from guilt, a beaking nose whose size belied
its wearer's years, and downy cheeks too soft
to match the squaring chin they crowned. This man-

child sighed, apologized for his offense,
and asked his parents for their counsel: "When
I finished all your business, Father, at
the Wells', I started back for home right off,
but out on the Vienna Road, I saw
a tent erected in the southern field
and heard a preacher there. I paused to catch
what he would say but then his congregants
began to shout and scream and drowned him out.
You wanted me at home, I knew, but they—
those folks were screaming like they fell into
a fire! And I was scared and thought they might
need helping, so I ran to see." With this
defense of his delayed return, the boy
expressed frank sorrow for the worry that
his dalliance had caused. He also asked
for leave to give a more detailed account
of all that he had seen and heard so as
to clarify his own inchoate grasp
on what had happened: *Why the wailing? How
had seizures led to Jesus?*

Father turned:
Mother assenting, Joseph painted them
a portrait of the pastor standing tall
and gaunt, surrounded by a double rank
of prostrate figures, towering above
them as a lonely mountain pine singed black
by lightning rises lordly over all
its neighbors which were felled by heaven's flame,
surviving still, in char. He told them of
the promise that perfection could be found
on earth and saw his older siblings stare,
astonished at the thought. The younger ones,
whose joy and hope had yet to be cast down
by Calvin, failed to see a reason for
excitement, but when Joseph startled from
his chair and Hallelujahed twice or thrice,
in imitation of the groaners' great
resurgence, everyone from Alvin down
to Carlos found the sight so funny that

for weeks the cry of "Hallelujah!" could
incite a chorus of good cheer. He closed
his recitation by reviewing each
alleged theophany, unconsciously
accentuating the diversity
of every vision's version of the form
of God—full half of which portrayed him as
ineffable, ethereal, a Lord
of Lords unknowable; the other half
described a Christ consumed with wrath, now come
in blood-stained robes to castigate the world,
a King of Kings unloveable.

When all
was said and Joseph's voice had trailed into
the autumn twilight, there was silence for
about the space of half a minute. It
was broken by the tongue of Mother Smith,
a little member of the human race
whose unimposing size disguised both strength
and outsized influence. Her five-foot frame
held every eye as she responded to
her son's report: "Joseph, your credulity
in counterfeited spiritual gifts
distresses more than it surprises. Fools'
gold gleams too bright to be ignored, but you,
my son, are no raccoon. Beware the wares
this blessed trickster sells; the promises
extended by these roaming peddlers of
religion never pay in full. They pass
from town to town and preach perfection, preach
destruction, preach whatever will excite
a crowd; and once some ten or twenty souls
have formed a flock, this shepherd leaves to find
the one, abandoning his ninety-nine.
So even if I thought that he would make
you his one hundredth—which I don't—his care
for you would come at the expense of those
he's left half dead and half alive beside
the road to Jericho."

So spake the wife
and mother to her husband and his name-
sake, both of whom gave grave attention to
her warm invective on the wickedness
of wanderers who lead their sheep in ways
not true. Indeed, the husband would have let
his wife's opinion stand as his but for
the boy's appeal to him: "And Father, what
are your thoughts?"

Joseph Senior shook his head
and let a playful grin unwind across
his face: "You children know that I hold no
opinions save the ones your mother does.
But if you want me to repeat herself,
I will. This Methodist itinerant
claims ten of his adherents now exist
in a perfected state; observe these ten,
their lives, their thoughts, their words and deeds, and see
if they obey God's law, persisting in
the hope you heard them share today. And if
their works reflect true faith, the words that led
them to this course must then be good; for by
their fruits shall they be known. But if their works
are those you might expect of any man
disposed to sloth and greed and lust and wrath;
if Thomas Auld persists in chasing girls
and kissing them or steals from the McBrides,
I think it will be safe to say that his
perfection has been overstated by
this pastor—this sly wolf in sheep's attire.
Religionists like him know no more of
God's kingdom than a common man who reads
the Bible regularly; maybe less.
Until that year when God's peculiar church
makes its appearance once again, therefore,
don't place your faith in ministerial
communications. Study scripture, and
compare its words with exhortations by
clergy from every sect. Those matching the

example of Christ's apostolic church,
examine more minutely, but, let no
excitement cloud your judgment. Join no church
until divine approval sanctions your
decision."

So replied the father to
his son's wholehearted question, ending with
this utterance his deviation from
routine. Renewing former inquiries,
the patriarch turned next to Hyrum, then
Sophronia, leaving Alvin till the last.
Yet Alvin's answer never marked the close
of this examination; parents, too,
confessed themselves accountable to God,
responsible for using heaven-sent
and home-baked daily bread to let their light
so shine before the children, that they might
both see and follow an example of
good works performed with quietness. In front
of their assembled offspring, Father first
asked Mother to recount her day (a task
with which Don Carlos, whose assistance formed
the half of all her labor, gladly helped).
Then Mother gave in turn the question to
her questioner, and only after they
were through did Alvin fetch the Bible from
a cedar chest where it lay snug. He brought
the Word to where his father sat and gave
it up into his care, then crouched beside
his siblings as they waited for the voice
of God to sound a benediction on
their day.

With bluff expression, Father Smith
began The Gospel of St. John: *In the*
beginning was the Word, and words were God,
and without words was not anything made
that was. And God is life, and God is light,
and God is flesh, but man has yet to see
the Father. John's good news continued, but
the boy's auricular attention waned.

His mind remained in orbit round the words
he had already heard—the Bible's words;
his parent's words; the words of sinners saved
from sin; the words of that itinerant
evangelist, which staggered Joseph in
the middle of the road of life. So deep
in thought was he that Joseph failed to hear
his father finishing the chapter with
John's promise, *Ye shall see the Son of Man.*

Their night complete, the children formed a line
and shuffled past their keepers for a kiss
before retreating to a counterpane
whose chill made sleep a slow affair. It was
an hour until deep breathing freed the pair
to whisper in the dark alone—as much
as you can be alone in any two-
room cabin sleeping ten. "My dear?" she asked.

"Uh-huh," he answered.

"Were we wrong to speak
so freely? Joseph seemed quite taken with
the Methodist approach. Should we have held
our tongues?"

"He would have found out how we feel
in time. A secret can't be danced around
indefinitely, like a maypole. And
besides, home is the place where, when you ask
a question, they should have to tell you truth,
no matter what. He ought to know that he
can trust us. He deserves that." Pause. "Should I
have said something about my dreams?"

"Tonight
was not the time, I think. You should, but wait
until it's just you two; an audience
of one allows both sides to speak without
restraint, and dreams like yours, gifts sent from God,
deserve the undivided mindfulness
of both a speaker and a listener.
Best not to trifle with the sacred, dear."

Their doubts expressed, advice dispensed, they closed
their eyes with soft goodnights. But Joseph lay
in bed awake, on this night as in nights
to come, attempting to distill a truth
from words fermenting in his brain, until
exhaustion overtook him and released
his mind to sleep's embrace. Awakening
each day renewed the search for that true vine
whose taste would slake his parching thirst for truth,
and Joseph, fairly running to and fro,
pursued the word of God wherever he
could find it. He attended Methodist,
Baptist, and Presbyterian events
alike. Indeed a Sunday often found
him in the congregations of all three
denominations, moving with young men
and women in a group from one place to
another, listening to preachers teach
and read and pray all afternoon, for hours.
Their voices rose and fell from dawn to dark,
like small, night-foundered skiffs kept anchored to
some seeming island, bobbing on the waves
but firmly bound to those beliefs which each
could claim distinguished his religion as
the only true and living church with which
the Lord was pleased. Joseph identified
the practices specific to those three
assemblies, hoping he would learn that one
could demonstrate a claim to absolute
authority with scriptural supports.

The Methodists, in keeping with his first
encounter, trumpeted the virtues of
perfection. Perfect love, they said, caused its
possessors to rejoice unceasingly;
give thanks in everything; and pray from noon
to night. What if, on rare occasions, their
devotions ended in the muscular
exertions criticized by some? Had not
the Psalmist said that *the zeal of thine house*
hath eaten me up? Then let such beware

lest they, too, anger God, as Michal when
she chastised David for his dance before
the Lord. Though Joseph little relished the
idea of thrashing on the ground, he could
not contradict the Bible; its command
to *be ye therefore perfect even as*
your Father in the heavens now is
perfect endowed the most remarkable
of Methodism's tenets with the seal
of sacred writ. Perfection was the nail
a Methodist could hang his hat on, and
though Joseph's cap had yet to find a home,
his restlessness had less to do with some
dissatisfaction at the notion of
a perfect man than with a chorus of
competing doctrines.

Elder Hartwell claimed
that God abhors the man who drinks a pint
or owns a slave and frequently condemned
"perfection" for its failure to exclude
practitioners of so-called social sins.
"A vice is not redeemed by public praise
or economic obligations," he
declared, and Joseph, who had read about
the Jubilee release of Israelites
and dietary laws for Nazarites,
discovered the impossibility
of proving someone right or wrong with no
help but the Bible. Elder Hartwell and
his Cold Water Society denounced
drinkers of coffee, tea, and alcohol
for "disregarding Christ's assurance that
a cup of water—cold, and given in
His name—could guarantee a man belonged
to Him."

Of course, the Reverend Beeston, whose
newspaper still ran ads for liquor, felt
obliged to rectify the errors in
his Baptist counterpart's assertion and,

with that intent, uncovered Noah's taste
for fine wines—an affinity, he said,
the Savior justified in Cana at
the feast, his first recorded miracle.
The Reverend castigated, too, the flock
of Minister McCleary, loathe to lose
his reputation as a critic who
believes in equal opportunity
by silently condoning Methodist
missteps. Ensconced within Palmyra's one
and only pulpit, he dispensed a dose
of old-fashioned determinism to
his congregants, admonishing the church
of dangers on its right and left, as old
man Mapple might have told the *Pequod*'s crew
that Moby Dick swam starboard and a snow-
capped squall blew larboard, if he, too, had shipped
longside the stranger we call Ishmael.

Because his mother's purchase of a pew
beneath the Reverend's eye entitled him
to front-row seats, young Joseph seldom missed
a sermon, stalwart in his search for truth
despite the somewhat pessimistic tone
that Beeston often took: "*To me belongs*
vengeance, and recompense; their foot shall slide
in due time: for calamity is nigh
at hand. Thus spake the Lord to Moses and
the wicked Israelites, to show how they
were constantly exposed to danger, kept
from falling in the pit by God's mere will
and pleasure only. But, when God's due time
arrived, they fell, inclined by their own weight
to Hell.

"In like manner the wicked of
our day abide in constant peril, with
the sword of justice brandished overtop
their heads at every moment, waiting to
descend and send them down to Hell to join
the legions writhing there, tormented by

the fierceness of his wrath. His anger, though,
is not confined to the impenitent
ingrates now castigated there; indeed
he doubtless is a great deal more upset
with many in this congregation, who
complacently sit here, than with the throng
already wracked below. For God is not
unmindful of your wickedness. The depths
are ready to receive you even now,
and your damnation slumbers not, nor sleeps.
Your unconverted souls traverse the pit
of Hell atop a rotten covering,
surrounded by innumerable points
too weak to bear your weight, too well obscured
to see.

"Beware those men who claim to know
a way across the fiery lake, who urge
you to rely on raised affections as
a sign of grace; the simple truth is that
enlightened minds, not raised affections, ought
to be the guide of those who seek for God.
Spontaneous emotion overflows
its bounds too often, and degenerates
almost invariably into base
displays of bestiality, without
regard for reason or religion. No;
no reveries so monstrous and absurd,
no acts so wicked and immoral as
those recently condoned by Minister
McCleary ever can be deemed divine
impulses justified by scripture. Such
attempts, to lull you into the belief
that God perfects his saints while still ensnared
in Adam's flesh, serve only to distract
you from a knowledge of your wretched state.

"Your wickedness gives you the heft of lead
and pulls you downwards with great weight towards
the pit; if God should let you go, you would
immediately plunge into the gulf,

and all your righteousness and prudence would
have no more power to prevent your fall
than spiderwebs have power to arrest
a millstone's plunge. The earth—she would not bear
your deviltry one moment were it not
God's sovereign pleasure. She is weary, pained
because of your iniquities, and longs
to be relieved of filthiness and sin.
You are a burden to creation, and
the sun does not dispense its light upon
you willingly, nor does the air you breathe
deliver life's sweet substance of its own
accord. Thus far the floods of judgment and
damnation have been kept in check, but you
are every day more guilty. Every day
the waters of his wrath increase. No more
postpone the day of your repentance, lest
an angry God grow weary of your pride
and open up his flood gates, sweeping you
to Satan's grasp, where all his savage strength
will tear and rend you for eternity."

With this and like encouragements to own
his fallen nature, Beeston urged the boy
to join the faithful, and if Joseph did
not come to Christ, at least he came to church.
McCleary, Hartwell, and the Reverend saw
him often, and his mother's Bible did
not see him less. As dry leaves rustled in
the wind, they rustled too in Joseph's grasp—
mere whispers of the thunderous words God spoke
to Moses on the mount; faint echoes of
the still small voice Elijah handed down
to Ezra. Bible leaves beneath his hands,
young Joseph spent the winter wandering
in black and white. White snowflakes wet upon
the ground, black tree bones bare against the sky,
the world revolved from day to night, each dark
more during than the one before, until
December twenty-third, when on the eve
of Christmas Eve, the sun began its north-

bound journey, shining like a new-made star.
So blackness grudgingly receded, and
the Smiths, as was their wont, assembled to
discuss the day's events and celebrate
with love the fourteenth anniversary
of Joseph's birth.

                                    No gifts announced his change
in age, but Mother Smith made raisin cakes
for all the family, and Father Smith
allowed his son to pick the passage they
would read that evening. "First Corinthians
thirteen," said Joseph, and the voice of Paul
presided at their celebration with
a discourse on the best gifts granted men:
faith, hope and charity. On faith, the stay
of priests and prophets; hope, that death may yet
prove merciful and brief; pure charity,
without which kings and chronicles and laws
will profit nothing. Fortified by Paul
and parents, Joseph faced his fifteenth year
in all of its uncertainty and could
not know the gnosis he'd receive before
his birthday next arrived.

                                    The new year came
like any other, at the old's demise,
and spring's bright hues replaced white winter's cold,
monochromatic constancy just as
they had for almost two millennia,
since life first bloomed eternal, in the night
of Bethlehem. Quite early in that turn
to spring, before the wood's first green was lost
and nature's new-curled golden flowers stretched
their leafy ribs, both Josephs worked the dirt,
beside each other, pulling out the gnarled
and twisted roots of trees cut down the year
before. But even though these stumps were dead
or dying, absent the appendages
empowered to draw life from light and lift
the whole to heaven, subterranean,

entangled networks lingered, squeezing stones
for water and compelling Joseph, next
his father, to attack them with an axe
and spade until a team of horses could
exhume them from their self-dug graves. They strained
to clear the field for planting, sowed the earth
with beads of sweat, and hoped the sun would give
them bread. Then when that orb descended, they
exchanged their hopes for bread in fact and picked
their way across the fields to Mother Smith's
awaiting supper.

As they walked, alone
while Alvin romped ahead with Samuel
and William, Joseph seized the circumstance
that left him with a parent's full and un-
divided attention; he spoke and asked
once more for patriarchal guidance in
resolving his denominational
dilemma:

"Father, in the past six months
I've listened to more sermons than . . . than all
the roots we wrestled from the ground today."

Holding an aching back, his father smiled
wryly. "My spine has sympathy for your
poor ears," he teased. "But why the furrowed brow?
Have you grown weary of the Reverend's voice?
I thought that you enjoyed attending all
those meetings."

"Well, I do, but . . ." Pause.

"But what?"

"But I had hoped by now that I would know
which church God wanted me to join—that some
scripture or sign would manifest his will
to me."

The laugh that left his lips seemed to
surprise the slumping farmer just as much

as Joseph Junior, who perhaps had been
offended if the laugher had not mused
aloud: "Impatient! So my Joseph has
become impatient . . . but, that is to be
expected. Even Peter, who had seen
the resurrected Lord, returned to nets
and fish when he grew tired of waiting for
the promised Pentecostal spirit to
arrive. The line between impatience and
an ardent zeal blurs quickly. I should know;
about ten years ago, I found myself
asking the questions you ask now. Like you,
I didn't know which church was right or how
to find the knowledge that I sought. I grew
disconsolate, then angry, at the lack
of guidance from a God who promises
to answer the importunate. I might
have lingered on in indignation if
your mother hadn't helped me through. She told
me, 'You know better than to reckon on
an answer from the God of Samuel
by such-and-such a time,' and finally
convinced me to accept God's timing as
a necessary stipulation of
receiving revelation. I resigned
myself to an indefinite delay,
not knowing when, or if, God would respond
to my entreaties for a knowledge of
His earthly church. But then, the very night
I made a resolution to accept
God's timing as my own, he visited
me in a dream.

"I rose and found myself
alone, surrounded by a ruined wood
on every side. The orchard—for it must
have been an orchard once—lay prone, its boughs
abjectly bowing to the ground's embrace.
No single cause had killed them all—on some,
the scars of sword or ax seemed gaping wounds;
on others, fiery tongues had licked the bark

off, leaving only char; still others showed
no signs of stress. An inward rot, perhaps,
had felled them, or fierce winds from off the sea.
No sound disturbed the quietude of this
arboreal boneyard, and I searched in vain
for signs of life amidst the graying wood's
decay. The trees stood still, as though transformed
to stone, a suffocated, dreary waste.
Perplexed, I knelt and prayed to understand
the orchard's import—*Why have I been sent*
to this forsaken place? The answer came
at once, a man in white who smiled and said:

"'This plot of ground was once the fairest and
most fruitful corner of my vineyard, but
you seek what now can only be found else
where. Travel south until you see a hill,
three miles from here, and on the westward slope
you'll light upon a fragrant cedar tree
new-fallen. Search beneath its limbs, and find
the box of stone that's buried there. It holds
the bread of life—which, if you eat it, will
impart the understanding you desire.'

"I carefully pursued the course he set
me, but as soon as I had tasted of
the manna in that box, a horde of beasts
rose up around me. Snapping turtles hissed
and spitting camels bared their yellow teeth,
while long-tusked boars laid waste to hedges. High
above me, eagles, hawks, and ravens filled
the sky with angry shrieks; beneath my feet,
the dirt erupted in a flood of mice
and moles and millipedes. It seemed that all
the unclean animals of Peter's dream
had suddenly turned savage and instead
of being eaten, now preferred to do
the eating. I, unwilling to become
their meal, escaped this menacing advance
by fleeing to the west, and three or four
times thought I had eluded their pursuit.

FIGURE 2. “The Dream of Joseph Senior.” Godwin.

But each time, after I had caught my breath,
that bestial mob would reappear and chase
me from my hiding spot. At last I chose
to turn and face my foes, to conquer or
be conquered—either one a better choice
than running endlessly. A brazen trump
spurred on the mob; an eagle dove, its beak
and claws . . ."

He stopped, but Joseph, now immersed
in the account, rebelled—demanded a
conclusion: "And the eagle? Did it rake
you, Father?"

"That's the pressing question, son.
I cannot tell you, for I do not know
myself; I woke before the bird had reached
me."

"So? What does it mean? The dream must have
a meaning, right?"

At this his father laughed
again: "My name is Joseph, but I'm not
that Joseph—and unless you are, we two
can only speculate about my dream's
interpretation."

But, before they could
confer and come to a consensus on
the question, little Mother Smith appeared
below the lintel, calling them to come
and eat. Her supper had a curious
effect upon them. Bellies full, they soon
forgot the spirit of frustration that
had driven their discussion, and instead
they reveled in the promised splendor of
the twenty-second chapter of St. John's
Apocalypse. They read of crystal streams
and trees whose fruit is ripe year round, of day
that never turns to dark and life that does
not end in death.

Some fruit is bittersweet.
The end of chapter twenty-two, the end
of Revelation, and the end of Christ's
New Covenant reminded them of the
mortality inherent in a world
still subject to the curse of Adam, one
whose origin and subsequent decline
the Smiths would study in the coming weeks
as they renewed their constant sojourn through
the Bible with the book of Genesis—
in the beginning. But for Joseph, the
beginning hardly seemed a place to find
his answers. The beginning was a place
to find more questions; answers were reserved
until the end, rewards for readers who
endured the epic march through Exodus,
Leviticus, and Numbers. Joseph had
already heard his father read the Good
Book through from Aleph to Omega, and
he felt that inspiration would arrive
more swiftly if he supplemented this
Old Testament agenda with his own,
more personal perusal of the New.
To that end, Joseph asked his mother's leave
to stay awake and read by candlelight,
and as the morrow was the Sabbath, she
agreed.

In opening the family's
large quarto Bible to a random page,
as Joseph generally did on these
self-guided forays into scripture, he
imagined that his fingers were inspired
to choose a chapter: hand-selected, as
it were, by Providence. That night, by chance,
the spine fell open near the end of Paul's
epistle to the Hebrews. *Let us run
with patience,* Paul admonished, echoing
the sentiment that Father Smith had shared
that afternoon, and Joseph, who could take
a hint as well as any other youth,

resolved at once to wait with patience for
the Lord to guide him in his search for truth.
That search continued slowly through the last
of Hebrews—hard words formed and re-formed by
an unlearned teen's still-halting tongue, with deep
and pregnant pauses interspersed throughout
for lexical digestion. By the time
he reached the end of Paul's epistle, these
delays occasionally stretched into
a fitful sleep, and Joseph would have gone
to bed but unexpectedly received
his second wind at the approach of James.
He read with reborn vigor till he found
the words he did not know he sought in verse
five: *If you lack for wisdom, ask of God,*
who loves to give, with open palms to all,
upbraiding not, and he will answer you.

II

In retrospect, it seemed so natural
to ask Heavenly Father for advice
directly, Joseph wondered he had not
already done so. Never had he knelt
in prayer, never addressed the God of Love
except through intermediaries like
the Reverend Beeston. Opening a fresh,
uninterrupted stream of discourse with
his Maker would recast the nature of
his interactions with creation, and,
he thought, *Why shouldn't I enjoy a new,*
original relationship with all
the universe? Why not discover true
religion in a revelation? God
has given me his word to answer and
disclose and open all; all this if I
will only ask and seek and knock!

He knelt
to pray, yet found himself unable to
articulate his want of wisdom with
the riptide snores of Senior sawing through
his consciousness like clock-work every six
seconds. Knees bent, he cast his eyes about
in search of some more silent corner of
the cabin but concluded quickly that
his only opportunity for peace
and quiet lay outside, away from the
reverberations of a nose whose size

and oblong cavities created an
acoustic space unrivalled till the rise
of Brigham's Tabernacle. Joseph left
their home and headed for the well; his tongue
felt thick and rubbery, but water would
relieve its sluggishness and help him to
address the Lord with eloquence. He walked
along a kind of corridor, the cows
chewing their cud intently on his right
and on his left, the wagon—

CRACK!

He felt
the first ball whistle past his fingertips
and heard the bullet thud behind him—heard
a bovine victim bellow at the bite
of lead. These sensory perceptions raced
through Joseph's nervous system to his brain,
and that deductive organ noted that
recorded data seemed consistent with
the symptoms of a gunshot, but, he, dazed,
stood still some moments, moving only when
the other shoe dropped, and he realized that
the shot was meant for him. He lurched back,

CRACK!

the second missile missing him by scant
inches as Joseph turned and sprinted for
the house. Inside, he roused his parents, who,
in truth, were half awake already thanks
to the report of the assassin's gun.
Incredulous at first, they listened to
his tale with fear. Then, trembling, they rejoiced
in the miraculous deliverance
of Joseph from his unseen enemies.
Determined to effect the physical
salvation of her children, Lucy pressed
her husband to wake Alvin and devise
a plan to rout the rifleman before
he could wreak havoc on their cabin. He

persuaded her of this scenario's
unlikely nature and convinced her to
accept the better part of valor as
the soundest principle on which to plan
resistance. Armed with naught but courage and
his cudgel, Father Smith assumed a post
beside the door, then waved his wife and son
to sleep. But guard-work grows monotonous,
and soon the poor man's feet rebelled. They led
him to a chair and bade him sit. He, loathe
to disobey, complied, and soon his eyes
made muster in the mutiny. They closed,
leaving the house with no defense save his
return to somnorific thunderings.

Outside? Outside, the grass grew damply chill,
and Caleb Howard staggered to his feet
from where he'd bedded, hidden underneath
the wagon. Low on liquid courage, his
desire to take revenge against the Smiths
came coughing to a stop, sobriety
and sanity returning slowly as
the engine of his inner devil seized
without its motive power. Howard shook
his head, disturbed that he had risked a swing
on gallows hill to claim his pound of flesh
for unpaid debt now four years old. So what
if Lucy left him short of Utica
with less to line his pockets than a man
might hope for? He had been prepared to do
the same to her, and killing crippled Joe
now seemed a silly way to salve his pride;
the only thing a corpse could buy him was
a hempen necktie, cinched too tight to suit
his taste. He wondered as he took his leave,
What demon had possessed me to behave
so?

Well, as Crankstool disentangled his
ethereal existence from the soul
of Howard with a sigh, he cursed the cold

return of incorporeality
and gnashed his teeth. But Caleb never heard
the dressing down he gave to Grumblebut,
a spectre charged with Howard's personal
damnation: "No mistakes with that one, dolt,
or Low Command will carve your ass in chunks,
stack 'em on spits, and serve you up as shish
kebab for supper in the mess hall. He's
as good as ours unless he gets a jolt
of camp religion. Men like Howard will
persist in sin until the day they wake
encircled in the welcoming embrace
of their true Brother Down Below. Just keep
the human happy with his pint of ale
and far away from those revivals. Most
men will do more to damn themselves and weak-
willed neighbors in the Enemy's own name
than any other way; the multitude
of churches is at present one of our
best assets, but the safest course to take
with loyal men like him is to preserve
their ignorance of *all* religion, false
though it may be."

Here Crankstool might have launched
into a dissertation on the great
divorce between the Church and churches, Christ
and crucifixes, but his audience
was growing antsy watching Howard's form
diminish in the distant darkness, so
he truncated his admonition to
the novice Temptor at a tenth of its
intended length and gave poor Grumblebut
the chance to extricate himself. Yet when
the weaker devil opened up his mouth
to speak, he found himself cut off at once.

"Still here?" snarled Crankstool. "I'm not flattered by
your insincere attentions to my rank.
If you have better things to do, then say
so; don't just stand there sniveling because
a Lesser Temptor on assignment from

the Lowerarchy happens to address
you. Now, be off, before I off you on
my own account!"

At Crankstool's feint towards
the pale-cheeked fiend, he cringed—then bolted to
the north in hot pursuit of Howard. With
a smirk of self-congratulation wrapped
around his face, the Lesser Temptor turned
away from Grumblebut's retreating shade,
already readying his speech for the
debriefing due to Seinvalore. He made
the half-mile journey from the cabin to
their designated rendezvous with time
to spare, astride a brisk wind blowing south-
southeast, a special perk reserved for those
about the Prince of Air's most pressing work.
But Crankstool had no time to revel in
this sign of his own self-importance; soon
as he set foot inside the chosen copse,
the stench of Seinvalore's sulfuric breath
besieged his nostrils.

"Listen, shit-for-brains:
whatever else you do or say in there,
don't start expounding on 'pure spirit' and
the 'pressure of the ordinary,' 'cause
if I catch heat for your pet theories, I'll
promote your kisser up to President-
in-Training of the scum that lick my boots,
and you can spend eternity with tread
marks on your tongue." Then Seinvalore stepped back,
assessing Crankstool's features with a grunt:
"At least you look half-way demonic." Close
again, more urgently, he whispered: "This
is big, could mean demotion for the both
of us, so don't forget your manners. If
they sit to honor you—"

But Seinvalore's
last piece of practical advice fell short
of the bewildered Crankstool's ears. He still

had no idea what Seinvalore had meant,
accosting him as soon as he stepped in
the copse, and lost all opportunity
to question the Inferior or hear
his final admonition when two strapped
thug-uglies, wearing the insignia
of Satan's privy council, came and dragged
him off, without a word of warning. Two
lone icebergs, bobbing in a pair of black
seas, each impaled by lightning, bracketed
his field of vision, steering Crankstool's sight
and feet. He marched through pines and other weeds
grown thick enough to stifle light. In cool
of night he walked, between twin brands upon
the shoulders of his captors, bracing for
an inquisition, there, among the trees.
No need for fig leaves; he'd done nothing that
the Glacietigni could object to. Why
the devils charged with Earth's destruction thought
a measly Lesser Temptor merited
such scrutiny he couldn't guess, but dreams
of falling into power drew him on.

As much as Crankstool had expected to
see Moloch, Loki, or Uriakeep—
some single representative of Low
Command's most humble body—nothing had
prepared him for the scene that met his view
when he emerged from out the underbrush
and shot into a clearing, still propelled
by his two minders.

Like Da Vinci's Christ,
surrounded by his Glacietigni, there
sat Satan, at a mossy oaken log
whose massive bulk divided this small space
devoid of undergrowth in two. Once green
and vital, tall as any other tree
surrounding (save the cedar that the Smiths
had cut the day before, whose stump now stood
between Satan and Crankstool, oozing sap

FIGURE 3. “Satan’s Congress in the Grove.” Godwin.

and water from the hatchet in its side,
where Joseph had secured, and left, his tool),
the fallen oak now teemed with termites, ants,
and other harbingers of inward rot,
its prone black bulk a husk of eminence
decayed. So Satan, sitting at the log
supremely unaware—and unaware
because supreme—of any irony
in his position, supervised the fiend's
debriefing personally, confident
his presence (an implicit threat of harsh
interrogation methods) would dissuade
the Lesser Temptor from dissembling.

"Did the boy begin his prayer?"

"Complete it?"

"How
did you distract him?"

"Is his zealousness
above the Sauline threshold?"

"Calculate
his martyr coefficient."

"Is he prone
to deep abstractions?"

"Will he pray again?"

The council's questions fell on Crankstool's ears
like body blows, jabs probing for the flaws
in Joseph's character and Crankstool's work.
He sparred with skill, massaging numbers to
produce the answers that he thought would please
them all and seemed successful, even grew
a little cocky in the seconds just
before that sucker punch connected with
his jaw.

The question, Satan's first and last,
his one inquiry—"Will he pray again?"—
knocked Crankstool cold. He understood the stakes

of such a question, for himself and for
the Smith boy too. The last time Satan had
shown interest in the prayers of an obscure
young man, the Son of God was crucified,
and Hell reaped such a surfeit of remorse
and sorrow, pain and anguish, that the stores
seemed inexhaustible, apparently
still undiminished after almost two
millennia of feasting. Crankstool knew
the boy was good as dead already, or
at least, like Job, would wish for death in lieu
of Satan's rabid wrath. As for himself,
Crankstool had the audacity to hope
that he could parlay his position as
the council's current link to Joseph, its
raison d'etre, into some more permanent
relationship, with all the privileges
that his demotion would entail. Before
the sound of Satan's voice had died from off
his lips, all this had flashed through Crankstool's mind
like lightning. Dazzling prospects, these abrupt,
but welcome, glimpses left him blinded twice:
first, whelmed with affirmation of his own
significance, and then, consumed by thoughts
of future glory.

                                    Lost in vanity's
labyrinth, Crankstool soon provoked the ire
of his interrogator, who assumed
the Lesser Temptor's silence was a sign
of perfidy. With mounting wrath, the first
to fall arose and towered over all
below. The tallest, broadest, fairest, most
imposing form of all God's sons lacked none
of its original perfection save
a light which issues from the eyes of all
who worship Elohim with singleness
of heart. Except for this, the visage of
that spirit formerly called Lucifer
remained unaltered, and except for this
the *David* wrought by Michelangelo

would do the deeds of its original.
The harrowed brow, the lips pressed tight, the vein
that throbbed within his neck: these signs betrayed
an anger bubbling up like molten rock
inside the Serpent, but his voice was cloaked
in velvet and concealed his venomed fangs
from view.

In *sotto voce*, Satan spoke,
reiterating his request: "I'll ask
once more. Do you believe the boy will try
to pray again?" But Crankstool never heard
the words, or hearing, failed to comprehend
their import, contemplating even then
rewards as yet unearned. To be ignored
not once but twice was more than Satan's pride
could bear; with one swift bound he hurdled past
the log that was his judgment bar and struck
the Lesser Temptor with a backhand stroke
which sent his insubstantial substance through
the air—his flight arrested by a more
particularly particled sylvain
of fir.

Then, ranting, stamping, Satan howled
above his victim: "Answer me!" He cursed
and kicked and clawed at Crankstool, who, it must
be said, at least had sense enough to know
resistance would be nocuous and lead
to greater efforts on the part of his
attacker. Crankstool also curbed the urge
to beg for mercy, lest he stimulate
the Snake's sadistic streak. Instead, he fell
to self-abasement, loudly pleading his
unworthiness so as to minimize
whatever satisfaction this abuse
provided his interrogator.

"Thank
you, Lowest of the Low—I am not fit
to be the object of your thoughts, much less
the target of a personal assault!

You humble me too much; do not exalt
yourself—your office—by consorting with
the likes of me unnecessarily.
I am not worthy!" These and similar
self-deprecating comments issued forth
from Crankstool, underneath the subject of
his sycophancy, pleading interspersed
with groans and gasps and cries of pain.

At last,
hunger for adulation sated and
his wrath abated, Satan stood again—
again demanded satisfaction from
the Lesser Temptor: "Denizen, you know
your failure to respond with promptness to
the questions asked you by myself, your Least
Executive, concerning Smith's attempt
at prayer, is tantamount to treason, and
it constitutes a clear and present threat
to our republic. Answer now and spare
yourself the capital displeasure of
the people, or resign the right of due
process and face summary judgment by
the legally elected officers
before you."

Crankstool, still with hopes his tongue
might extricate him from his current straits,
and not confiding overmuch in rights
or processes, relied instead on law,
on Crankstool's own first law of pride, in fact,
which held that egos set in motion tend
to stay in motion, following the path
of highest praise without regard for their
trajectory or destination. Like
the music of a pungi, Crankstool's voice,
both grating and ingratiating, rose
with reedy importunity to plead
its master's cause, and prove his theorem too:
"The glory of your presence underwhelmed
me, Humble Tovarishch. Your circumspect

demeanor and the muted tones in which
you spoke; your patience with my questioners
(who failed to ask the vital thing) and me
(who failed to answer); your superior
physique, concealed until sheer urgency
made modesty a lesser virtue: all
contributed to my paralysis
when you addressed me first. How to respond
to such deliberate elocution, such
reluctant leadership? Though all in Hell
are equal, all acknowledge you are more
than equal; and, as there is nothing so
unequal as the equal treatment of
unequals, how was I to answer your
address? Thus, lost in contemplation of
your selfless service and perfect example,
not knowing whether I should speak to you
according to your artificial, though
sincere, pretensions to equality
or with the deference naturally due
your low desserts—thus, I neglected to
disclose the information you had asked
of me. Yes, Joseph will assuredly
attempt to pray again, tomorrow night
if not before. If you intend to stop
him or to redirect his energies
in less ascendant enterprises, haste
is needed."

Crankstool stopped, and Satan smiled,
baring his teeth with wolfish appetite.
At this, the Lesser Temptor shrank, afraid
his flattery had failed; but martyrs love
to be confirmed in their own sense of self-
determined singularity above
all else, and heaven's first martyr was no
exception. Joseph was the object of
his gluttonous grin, and Crankstool's error had
already been forgotten by the Snake.
Without another thought for Crankstool—who
retreated, unimpeded, to observe

the scene in relative obscurity,
behind the trees that ringed the clearing—and
with palpable emotion, Satan turned
to face the council.

"Since we slew the Son
and his apostles and assumed control,
through Constantine, of church government, we
have known this day would come, that one year our
Great Enemy would make another bid
for power, jealous as he is, as he
admits to being, even of our poor,
modest demesnes among his numberless
infinities of worlds. Although we foiled
his previous attempts—the Lutheran Ruse,
the Muslim Gambit—those coulés were feints,
not passes truly seeking to restore
hegemony. The Smith boy represents
our first rencounter since the Son's ascent"—
Which overturned the devils' false belief
that flesh and blood are universally
subjected to their grave decrees, but which
had also left the vast majority
of souls under their sway intact; and what
good shepherd muses on a single lost
Lamb when the ninety-nine lie hobbled safe
within the valley's shadows, shielded from
the sun's bright rays?—"and we must make a show
of power, demonstrate that humankind
are subject still and always unto Death
and Hell. This Joseph, like the first, is meant
to raise a servile nation: subjects for
the Tyrant, who, unlike the people of
Melchizedek and Enoch, whose entire
aim was escaping us, will seek instead
to overthrow our humble enclave of
equality and annex it for him
who is already omnipossident
otherwise. Not content with herds and flocks
of numberless expanse and infinite
variety, he covets that which we

possess, our one, our only little ewe
lamb, Earth. Make no mistake: In Smith we face
an existential threat. Although the boy
has yet to lift his voice in prayer, much less
his arms in combat, we have no choice but
to strike preemptively, to undermine
his power to wage war in future and
defend our world from gravest danger. If
the Tyrant has elected to enlist
women and children in the vanguard, he
alone must answer for the casualties
incurred, for these and all atrocities
against the people he pretends to love
so much. The advent of our ancient foe
from heaven, Zachiel, was written in
the stars some fourteen years ago, and Thoth
assures me that this Joseph is the one
foretold, the seventh and the last of our
Great Enemy's archangels to receive
a body. Even the Almighty has
a limited supply of champions
with which to challenge our dominion in
this realm of matter, and if we can claim
a conquest over Zachiel—this Smith
boy—we will have withstood the Tyrant's last,
best hope of conquering this haven from
his heavenly control. Our object, then,
is this: to do with Smith as we have done
with every agent of imperial
ambition. How to thwart, destroy, distract,
deceive, or otherwise dissuade him from
accomplishing the will of Heaven? That,
distinguished comrades, is the question you
must answer and the reason I convened
this congress."

Like the angler hidden in
a bush's leafy depths to shield himself
from both the unsuspecting fish he seeks
to hook and the more vigilant, if less
than honest, eyes of wardens who themselves

enjoy a bass fillet or pan-seared trout
whenever they believe the master's gaze
is elsewhere, Satan trod with tact where none
was needed, speaking to his most depraved
companions with that same calumnious art
that first seduced them from the Father's side,
as if he could no longer separate
himself from the façade of righteous ire
and indignation he had worn so long,
to such effect. But if this serpent seemed
intractable, unable to evolve
and far less flexible than exegetes
or herpetologists might have supposed,
his councilors were just as firmly fixed
in former ways. All present understood
that Satan would eventually be sent,
alone, to face the Smith boy, as he had
been sent so many times already—to
the Son, to Job, to Adam—although each
successive trial seemed less fruitful than
the one before.

But nonetheless, they all
would play the parts that they had acted out
in every iteration of that first
demonic council one more time. The same
three fiends would speak again—brash, bellicose
Moloch, the softly slothful Belial,
and avaricious Mammon—plus a fourth,
Erotika. (Her elevation to
this speaking role came only when she learned
that Adam had rebuffed and Eve embraced
temptation; she then raised Hell's feminine
minority—all twelve point five percent—
in protest of the Lowerarchy's glass
floor. She demanded that those epithets
for female spirits—*Daughter*, *Sister*, *Wife*,
Mother—be stricken from the records and
replaced with terms identifying them
as independent agents loyal to
the Revolution—*Temptress*, *Demoness*,

She-Devil, *Bitch*, etc.—and that
the constitution be amended to
establish an equality of rights
without regard for gender; women's rights
have never been so popular on Earth
as Eve's transgression made them, then, in Hell.
Thus, when the Glacietigni next convened,
the night of Abel's baptism, she joined
that body as its thirteenth member and
advised, on that occasion, incest: foul
seduction by Eve's daughters.) Each debate,
a ritual: the same four fiends would speak;
Beelzebub would ask a volunteer
to take the mission on; and Satan would
stand forth to offer up his services,
reluctantly.

No change in Hell, where back-
room politics would shape the outcome in
this hundred-and-eleventh council as
they had in the original. No need
for some new secret combination when
the first had worked so well; far better to
maintain the status quo with hackneyed, stale,
run-of-the-mill tongue-wagging than disrupt
traditions with predictable returns
on investment for novel words of an
exotic derivation. Why pursue
things unattempted yet in prose, when few
of those in Hell who'd learned to read would make
the trip—no middle flight—to archives where
the meeting's minutes would decay, in far
Bibliadurus, knowing fewer still
would have the patience, time, and skill to parse
such records and admire rhetorical
refinements made throughout the years? Each spoke,
without an audience, at present or
in future, not for fame but from a sense
of duty to a nation and a way
of life besieged by what appeared to be
an overwhelming power: Belial,
Mammon, Erotika, and Moloch.

FIGURE 4. “A Council of Devils.” Godwin.

With
a languid grace and smile urbane, that first
arose to speak again in favor of
ignoble ease: "Emergencies, dear friends
and colleagues, seldom seem more urgent than
when hasty, desperate measures meant to end
a conflict fail, inciting panic in
the hearts of those who lose the battle and
emboldening its victors. Tactical
defeats destroy morale, but tactical
retreats advance strategic purposes.
They breed complacency within our foes.
No sense preparing plans for an attack
in which success seems dubious at best;
omnipotence must be massaged, out-flanked,
not openly assaulted. Like a small,
innocuous animalcule whose full
potential as an agent of disease
can only be unlocked by contact with
an antipharmic that attacks it and
provokes the germ to mutate into some
more deadly, more resilient version of
itself, this Smith boy is a dormant threat,
a muscle-bound pubescent fraction of
the spirit who commanded heaven's hosts,
and nothing will restore his former strength
and pugnative demeanor faster than
our opposition. Even if he prays,
what worst could happen? Say the Tyrant deigns
to answer—which he seldom does—and makes
the boy a second Samuel; some Saul
or David will defect and nullify
his contribution to the heavenly
campaign. Or say he somehow finds, decodes,
and prints the golden Bible buried now
inside Cumorah—not a likely feat;
Herr Gutenberg, Jerome, and John will all
conspire to damn the boy for adding to
the words of Revelation. Outcomes so
wildly improbable are hardly worth
averting; haven't Heaven's miracles

been met with apathy in every age?
Reforms, initiated in response
to the miraculous, decline and fail
because the mortal flesh our Foe's so keen
on cannot hold an edge unless it's kept
in constant contact with the grindstone, and
one prayer, whatever its immediate
effect, can have no lasting impact on
the boy's development; he will forget
and soon return to foolish errors, to
the weaknesses of youth and foibles of
his human nature. Sacrifice this pawn.
Permit his prayer, and we will soon recoup
attendant short-term losses. But, if we
contest it, fearing present costs, we risk
awakening a spirit foreordained
to curb our freedoms—risk creating that
same enemy we plot now to destroy."

To which the crusty Mammon made his now
traditional rejoinder: "To propose
procrastination seems appropriate
if in the service of some larger plan,
but Belial's indefinite delays
sound too much like our potent Enemy's
own propaganda, like Gamaliel's
soft, optimistic fatalism. Our
best interests must be earned, not languidly
awaited. Let us speak of dividends,
discharging prejudice against the gold
plates of Cumorah. Nothing will destroy
the poor and innocent more quickly than
discovering some brave new world of wealth,
and I suggest that we allow the boy—
even encourage him—to search until
he finds the record. Poverty will lead
him to regard those golden leaves for their
pecuniary, not veridical,
potential, and the Tyrant—who detests
all those that seek to profit from the sale
of sacred gifts, as Simon Magus might

attest—should be enraged enough at his
idolatry to disavow the boy
entirely, even strike him dead. And if
Joseph somehow survives this first, innate
attraction to the earth that gave him form
and substance, want will soon convince him that
it were no sin to use his talents to
discover other treasures, buried for
less holy purposes. No man who's seen
the gleam of gold emerging from the ground
can ever be content to till the land
for daily bread; a money-digger once,
a money-digger always. Let him find
the record; let him try to reconstruct
the blessed state that it describes and build
Utopia. Those plates will bind him to
our cause as firmly as the golden nail
that fastened Hebrew servants to the door
post of their master's house—no place so sure
to foster greed as paradise. A poor
young man wants nothing more than to grow up
a rich old man, but poverty promotes
humility unless persuaded that
prosperity is possible. The love
of money will afflict him, as it pained
poor Solomon, but only if he learns
to trust in gold—and solitary weeks
spent reading and recording stories that
are written on the stuff will teach him to
regard that metal as a sacred source
of safety and society."

He sat;
Erotika rose next and turned to face
the hardened members of that devilish
assembly with a mocking smile: "I see
no reason to expose this record to
the peepings of a boy who drives the plough.
Do men want *nothing* more than gold? As I
recall, the deviance of Solomon
had more to do with how he spent his wealth

than an unnatural attraction to
the jewels and precious metals that comprised
it. To be sure, he built a temple for
the Tyrant, but, being a democrat
at heart, he broadened that first ritual
embrace of Yahweh to include diverse
religious voices representative
of all the cultures and ethnicities
within his kingdom and erected halls
of worship for each one of us as well.
Must I remind you of the cause for this
enlarged conception of the sacred? Look
no further! Certainly not lust for gold—
no need to send him rooting in a dirt
hole for the mines of Ophir when the boy,
like Solomon and every other man,
would so much rather plumb the fleshy depths
of female . . . hearts. Forget the shafts extolled
by Mammon's metal fetish, and reflect
instead on that great boon our Enemy
bequeathed us in the feminine mystique,
that antipole to which the needles of
men's inner compasses are magnetized.
No reason to reorient the boy's
worldview by rubbing this gold Bible in
his face as though it were a lodestone which
could make him come to our side; he just needs
a sextant whose anatomy will help
interpret the external workings of
that compass—needs an Eve whose wanton curls
and murmuring lips will hale the eye and bid
a man forsake his God. No—better yet,
a host of women eager to assist
him in the labor of delivering
the Tyrant's children and fulfilling his
command to multiply. Ask Abraham
how well the handmaid Hagar shared a bed
with Sarah. Press that liar, Jacob, as
to whether a plurality of wives
promotes familial peace and unity.
Most marriages transform the beautiful

to commerce and dissension in less time
than rutting animals require to pledge
their mutual affection; bigamy
just guarantees the process, and if we
can introduce contemporary role
models whose rationales for wedding more
than one woman will give him cover, lust
will prove the boy's undoing."

With a voice
less certain than insinuating, she
trailed off, as though she were unwilling or
unable to escort her logic to
its climax; Moloch, stiff and tumid, like
his peers, from sitting rigidly erect
so long, shot up as soon as she had done
and glared disdainfully at each of those
who had already spoken as he paced
frenetically across the clearing—once,
twice, thrice—before erupting into speech:
"Have we learned nothing from the Enemy's
last great assault? This half-assed shit just does
not work! If we expect to stop that boy
from winning here on earth the war he waged
against us while in heaven, then we can't
content ourselves with sowing seeds of sin
as though he were some second Eutychus;
another Ananias; or a male
companion for those silly women Paul
condemned. Among the feeble masses, such
an emphasis on peccadilloes—sly
inertness, greed, and lust—might satisfice.
But Zachiel, if this is he, has zeal
enough for fifty men and cannot be
expected to abandon heaven's cause
because he sees some wench with shiny hair
or finds a bit of buried gold. To hear
you talk, the boy has less in common with
the spirit whose swift daggers drove us down
to Hell than with a color-blind raccoon
that can't resist the trapper's bright tin bait,

and to ensnare him all we need are lures
of a sufficient size and luster. Don't
delude yourselves! Whatever weaknesses
our over-zealous cousin has acquired
with his new flesh, a wandering eye is most
assuredly not one of them. As his
refusal to accept the platitudes
with which we've always pacified the poor
and pious demonstrates, this Joseph can
discern between the coin of heaven and
our counterfeit; what's more, his lust for God
is such as twixt a miser and his wealth
is found. His eyes are fixed on heaven, and
he wouldn't even see, much less forsake
his faith to follow, your intended lures
of leisure; treasure; pleasure. Rather than
attempt to turn his tunnel vision to
another end, we would be wiser to
exploit the lack of parallax that mars
the sight of single-minded souls. All filled
with thoughts of heaven, he will scarcely pause
to question whether his Cyclopean
aggression may have executed God's
titanic will before the latter days
demand—until his proud and pugnative
demeanor, galled to rage by our assaults
against his character and followers
and cause, erupts in wrath and oversteps
the limits of his Master's leash with bold,
offensive sallies. Thus, by goading him
with countless minor cruelties of the kind
our Enemy so unrealistically
expects his servants to endure without
complaint shall we, at length, incite the boy
to some vain shows of military might
unauthorized by heaven. Demagogues
will slander him as an American
Mohammed seeking to convert, debauch,
and subjugate by sanguinary means,
and every freeman in the land will fight
with us against the restoration of

a tyrant governing by 'divine right.'
Without the arm of heaven to sustain
his sword or popular opinion to
protect his reputation, we can cut
him down like a green, unripe thistle when
we please, and certainly before the sharp-
barbed blossoms of his gospel can disperse
too broadly. Let us make a martyr of
him; neither hagiography nor the
idolatry that martyrs always breed
are antithetical to our designs.
But more importantly, a soldier can't
surrender: if we want to neutralize
this last great threat, the boy must die."

The war-
monger retreated, sat, and Hades nudged
Beelzebub back into consciousness.
He hadn't heard the whole debate, but then,
he knew his lines by heart and answered each
of the preceding speakers perfectly,
according to their character, before
expounding on the need for one among
them to prevail in single combat with
this slave of the Almighty, as a proof
of their superiority. A roll-
call vote approved his motion unopposed,
and Lucifer was nominated for
the task, an invitation he took up
reluctantly—as always. Then, adjourned,
the council members went their separate ways,
to wait their Least Executive's next call.

III

Faint light—not luminous enough to steer
a single eye, but still sufficient to
direct the feet of one whose vision is
attuned to darkness—guided Crankstool's flight
as he retraced the path he'd taken from
the Smith's log cabin to his rendezvous
with Seinvalore and Satan, who had found
the Lesser Temptor trying to escape
the council unobserved and collared him,
then commandeered his service with a charge
to roust the Smith boy and deliver him
back to the clearing. Crankstool reached the house
while Lucy's boys were yet abed, and he
began a search for decoys that might draw
the youth outside the safety of his home,
that institutional extension of
the heavens into which no devil may
advance without an invitation. Soon,
he heard a bovine answer to his quest
reverberating from the barn. It was
still very early in the morning, but
with cows to milk and other pre-dawn chores
to tend to, Crankstool knew the Smiths would not
be long in stirring.

Sure enough, the door
swung open minutes later, and the three
oldest boys—Alvin, Hyrum, Joseph—all
emerged, half stumbling, half asleep, into

the April air. Behind a smoky bank
of clouds the newly waning gibbous moon
still shone with unremitting radiance,
but not a trace of that reflected star
light pierced the misty darkness that obscured
the Smiths' abode; the trio made its way
toward the cowshed led by nothing but
the quaking glow and fragrant odor of
a single spermaceti candle. Once
inside, the younger two, astride their stools,
began to tug at turgid udders while
their elder brother mucked each stall and forked
fresh hay atop an empty manger. For
a time the only human sound to mar
the early morning stillness was the hack
of phlegm relocating from throat to floor,
but this somatic cleansing seemed to rouse
the boys, at last, from slumber. Joseph spoke
and told his brothers of the night's events—
how he had gone for water; how the gun's
first sharp report awakened him to all
the perils of his present state; and how
kind providence had caused him to retreat
scant seconds prior to the second ball's
coming.

With grateful voice grave Hyrum gave
a prayer of thanks, but Alvin laughed and said,
"Next time you think a murderer's outside
the house, you're carrying the light." And then,
more somberly, he warned, "I'm guessing that
the gunman's up and gone since no one shot
us as we crossed the yard, but we'd be fools
to cross again without confirming that
he's left." They peered with caution at a world
all bathed in gray, as dawn began to stalk
the day, and minutes later Hyrum found
the bed of smothered grass whence Howard had
decamped the night before. They squatted there,
and squandered breath in speculation while
the demon labored to convince a squirrel

that acorns lay concealed beneath a stack
of kindling. When its scrabbling claws dislodged
a stick, the Smith boys startled at the sound,
imagining their would-be killer had
returned for blood; seeing the squirrel, they laughed
at their collective folly—the idea
of fearing such a creature! Alvin joked
that even if the pint-sized rodent had
a hatchet or some other weapon, just
their toes would be in danger—jesting words,
but they reminded Joseph of his own
tool, rusting in the cedar stump. He told
both brothers of his fault and reassured
them that he would be cautious as he fetched
the hatchet; then, without responding to
their protests, he arose and jogged off at
the rising of the sun to meet the Prince
of Darkness and to ask the question whose
reply has since been heard around the world.

Wrenching his hatchet from the bark where it
was buried, Joseph lost his footing on
the forest's slimy sub-floor of decayed
organics, tumbling backwards. As he sat,
he noticed that the normal sylvan sounds
seemed to have disappeared; remembering
his futile quest for peace and quiet just
the night before, the boy decided to
renew that first attempt at prayer and knelt
beside the stump.

"O God in heaven—" he
began, but gagged, his tongue engorged and dry,
as darkness deep enough to drown in draped
his body like a second skin and filled
his mouth with ash. His constitution strained
against an unseen adversary's choke-
hold—nostrils wide, snorting for air, more horse
or hog than human; muscles firing blanks
at spectral shadows; ears unable to
ignore or process all the tortured screams
and other aural horrors fighting for

a corner of his consciousness. Oppressed
by foreign powers, Joseph struggled to
establish his autonomy and with
some effort managed to stop rolling on
the forest floor as though he were a sea-
sick barrel crossing the Atlantic in
a schooner's hold, determined not to let
external stimuli deprive him of
his agency.

For his part, Satan took
the boy's abrupt quiescence as a sign
of his surrender and began to gloat
over the prostrate aspect of his prey.
A moment later, though, when Joseph raised
his head up off the ground, contempt gave way
to shock, and that surprise caused Satan to
release his stranglehold just long enough
for Joseph to regain his feet. Their war
resumed at once, and Joseph stepped toward
the stump to brace himself against the weight
of Satan's brutal onslaught. His left leg
buckled first. Crawling on his knees, he went
a little further, falling on his face.
Despair sank in, and Joseph stretched his hands
as though in supplication for the end;
his fingers found a root, then—

Light, more felt
than seen, descended from the heavens and
delivered him immediately from
the enemy that held him bound. He rolled
over and saw the treetops bathed in flames
far brighter than the noonday sun, white tongues
of fire illuminating every bush
and branch without consuming even their
most tender, curling leaves. This radiant blaze
above drew gradually nearer till
it rested on the boy. Enveloped by
that brilliant sphere of flame, his mind was caught
away from contemplation of the sights
and sounds surrounding, and he found himself

FIGURE 5. "The Opening of Joseph's Vision." Godwin.

wrapped up in visions of the heavenly
Jerusalem, whose jasper walls were thronged
with an innumerable company
of angels singing praises to the Lamb.
Concentric circles of the faithful danced
with upraised arms around the ramparts, and
their fingers twirled together through the air,
revolving like the tasseled hem of some
divinely skirted whirling dervish or
the spray of water droplets sluicing off
a miller's wheel. Four rivers streamed like spokes
from under a quartet of thrones arranged
at cardinal points around a central square,
and Joseph watched with wonder as a pair
of personages left their garden thrones
together and descended slowly to
him. Clothed in searing light that seemed to bake
a filmy membrane off his corneas,
both luminescent bodies braked above
him in the air, afloat, and Joseph saw
with some surprise that these two Beings shared
a single face, physique, and wardrobe—that
the two were one. They stood there silent and
unmoving save the whisper of their robes,
which billowed gently in the breeze as though
they had been cut from clouds, expectantly.

After a brief delay, remembering
his purpose, and pastoral battles for
the Bible's apostolic sanction, and
the lack of Christian union, Joseph screwed
his courage up and blurted out, "Which church
is right? In which should I enlist?"

The Man
whose face seemed slightly more supernal, like
it formed a mold from which the second had
been cast—his pupils sparkled, and he spoke,
with bared arm pointing to the figure at
his right before declaring: "Joseph, this
is my Beloved Son, in whom I am
well pleased: Hear him."

The other personage
stepped forward, gliding softly down to earth,
and stood before the boy with open palms.
In his divinely reconstructed hands—
hands that had labored, built, and healed without
expecting compensation—Joseph saw
the nail prints left by Judas' lynch mob, and
his own hands suddenly felt slippery
with blood. Tears sprang unbidden to his eyes
as he reflected on errata, sins,
and follies wrung out drop by bloody drop,
from every pore, on his account. With fear
and trembling Joseph struggled to his knees
and bent to kiss the broken feet. He wept
with wracking sobs of painful joy and bathed
each scar in guilt and gratitude and love.
The knees above him flexed, and Joseph felt
a gentle touch which quelled his crying and
invited him to lift his gaze.

Two ears,
two eyes, a nose, two lips: he had a face
like every man but one in which no trace
of pride or jealousy or fear appeared,
a canvas where opposing virtues met
their mates. Compassion; judgment; wisdom; zeal;
humility; and strength: his countenance
expressed them all, and Joseph stared in awed,
mute adoration upwards, grasping his
forgiving palms as though to reassure
himself that flesh and bone had just revealed
the truth that Jesus was and is the Christ,
Son of the Living God.

A man, more sure
of his own place in the eternal plan,
would have been patient; Joseph, being but
a boy, was not. Now that he knew God's love,
he knew that God would keep his promises,
and so he asked again, expecting to
be given: "Which of all the sects is right?
the Methodists?"

Unbending at the knees,
the Lamb rose up a Shepherd and began
the work of gathering his wayward sheep:
"Joseph, my son, rejoice; in me your sins
have been forgiven. For behold, I am
the Lord of Glory, Jesus Christ: He who
was crucified for all mankind, that none
need suffer if they will repent. But all
those who will not repent must suffer just
as I, with pains that caused me, greatest of
God's sons, to tremble, bleed from every pore,
and plead that this, last, bitterest of cups
might be forgone. Nevertheless, I drained
the chalice of affliction so that all
those who believe in me and hearken to
my words may have eternal life.

"And now,
behold, the whole world lies in sin, and I
have looked upon its churches with contempt,
speaking of sects and creeds collectively,
not individuals. Do not attach
yourself to them, for they have turned aside
their hearts from following the precepts of
my gospel. Some seek earnestly for truth
but know not where to find it, led astray
by others, who draw near me with their lips
yet scorn me in their hearts. All these corrupt
professors teach for doctrine the ideas
of men, to gratify their pride. They have
impoverished the faith of millions, and
mine furor has been kindled over the
inhabitants of Earth. According to
the wickedness of their endeavors I
will visit them in judgment and will bring
to pass the sifting spoken of by all
my prophets and apostles.

"Nation shall
contend with nation, and there shall be wars
and rumors of wars; great pollutions shall
envelop Earth, and murders, whoredoms, and

deceivings shall prevail. There shall be heard
reports of earthquakes, tempests, fires, and clouds
of smoke in foreign lands. Men's hearts shall fail
them, and the love of many shall wax cold
because iniquity abounds. And in
that day the people shall be lifted up
in pride because of their great riches. For
there shall be many merchants, lawyers, and
officials, all distinguished into ranks
according to their wealth and chances to
obtain an education. And for this
inequity they shall be broken up
by jarrings, strifes, contentions—covetous
and lustful cravings. Brothers shall attack
their brethren; blood shall cover up the moon;
and then shall I come quickly to dispense
with egoism—clothed in judgment and
destruction.

"But before that day my strange
love shall work upon the hearts of many,
and I will pour my Spirit out upon
all flesh. Young women shall dream dreams; young men
shall hear my voice in prayer; and I will show
unto the world that I change not. I am
today the same as yesterday—the same
forever. Therefore, I will now proceed
to show a great and marvelous delight
among this people, either to convince
them of my gospel unto peace and life
eternal or convict the hardness of
their hearts and blindness of their minds until
they have been brought into captivity
by him who was and is the father of
all lies. My truth shall break across the earth
like roaring waves upon the shore, and you,
my servant Joseph, shall interpret for
this generation. Ere I formed you in
the womb, I knew you, and before you left
the belly I ordained and sanctified
you as a prophet to the nations.

"You
shall be my voice of warning to the world
and cry repentance unto presidents
and rulers, rich and learned, for they have strayed
from all my ordinances and believe
in incorrect doctrines, persuaded by
the Evil One to walk in their own ways
and after idols of their own conceit,
from dimness into darkness. Wherefore, I,
the Lord, have called you, Joseph, to proclaim
these things, that faith might be increased upon
the earth; that every man might speak in my
name; that my everlasting covenant
might be established; that my only true
and living church might be erected on
a sure foundation. For when Satan shall
send forth his mighty winds and iron shafts
of war, my saints must see the storm's approach
from watchtowers and gather to a place
of refuge which shall never fall. The hearts
of fathers and the hearts of children shall
be turned to one another, and my house
shall once again be reared, that all my saints
might come into my presence to receive
my holy oracles and be endowed
with power from on high. Nevertheless,
the time is not yet come—the time when you
shall build my house. You cannot comprehend
the nature of that work which you will do
on my behalf in future days, but as
your understanding of my gospel grows,
and as you implement its principles
into your life, your power to discern
and to perform my will shall be increased.

"Go forth, and hearken to my counsel. We
shall visit you again, in days to come,
and give you new instructions."

Joseph woke,
uncertain how much time had passed since he
left home, uncertain where his hatchet lay,

uncertain how and when his life would change.
But one thing he was certain of: God loved
him. Jesus had forgiven him—no, He
had given for him all that was required
and had commanded him to qualify
for his commission, in the future, as
an under-shepherd. Joseph lay there, spent,
content to stare as spring unwound before
his eyes, indefinitely, only roused
by Alvin's voice. Prolonged exposure to
the light of Christ had given him a case
of bosom burn; heart palpitations and
core temperatures well north of normal left
him weak, and conscious of his weakness, he
let Alvin haul him to his feet.

On their
return trip Joseph told his brother how
he'd prayed; of wrestling with an angel; and
of meeting Jesus again, for the first
time, face-to-face. If Alvin was surprised
by Joseph's story, no stray word betrayed
him. Truth be told, his brother seemed to be
anticipating each successive plot
point, as though Joseph's basic narrative—
boy prays to God; devil deters boy; boy
persists; devil departs; and God names boy
a prophet—had been lifted from a best-
seller whose Everyman protagonist
would denouement in glory. (Novelty
was never an accomplishment or sign
of heavenly approval; Alvin knew
Ecclesiastes well enough for that.)
His probing questions and approving grunts
or nods seemed almost catechetical,
and this first, sympathetic audience
braced Joseph for the cynicism and
the scorn to come.

Arriving at their home
as Joseph brought his narrative to its
conclusion, Alvin told the prophet, "I

believe you, brother. And I thank you for
your confidence. However, I suspect
in coming days your witness will be met
with skeptic mockery. So cleave to your
convictions, and await the further light
and knowledge that was promised to you by
the Savior.

"In the meantime, don't cast pearls
before the swine; recall that Samuel
was loathe to tingle Eli's ears with news
that God had picked another prophet, and
he certainly did *not* invite King Saul
to Jesse's house for the anointing of
his eighth son. Reverend Beeston and the rest
probably won't embrace a vision that
denounces them as well-intentioned but
misguided frauds, especially if you—
a boy, unbaptized, with no better than
an elementary education—are
the visionary. I believe you, Joe,
but I'm your older brother; I'm supposed
to. Didn't Aaron follow Moses when
Jehovah called him from the burning bush
to challenge Pharaoh? All I'm saying is
that you don't have a rod, and Heaven seems
to think you need more seasoning before
we take on Egypt. So be careful who
you tell about this. Mother? Father? Fine—
but no one else, unless you're sure that God
would have you speak."

These providential words
of counsel were accepted with a nod
and grateful grin. But Joseph quickly learned
that keeping all these things locked in his heart
for pondering was far more difficult
than Mary made it seem. When Samuel
heard Joseph ask their parents for a word
in private, he decided that he *had*
to know his brother's secret and became
importunate, cajoling Joe with oaths

and promises of confidence. He prayed,
as Alvin had suggested, and was told
in no uncertain terms that Samuel
could not, as yet, be trusted to respect
the sanctity of revelation; truth
must dazzle gradually or every man
go blind, and patience is the better part
of prophecy more oft than not. And yet,
not yet implies a future change of heart,
so Samuel persisted. Joseph asked
a second time and got the same reply.
The third time, though—perhaps like Luke's unjust
judge, God had tired of Joseph's pleading; or,
perhaps he had, like heart-sick parents of
that prodigal, acceded to unwise
demands, instead of waiting till the youth
no longer valued his permission or
advice—the third time Father granted his
request: Sam *could* be told, provided he
agreed to hold this knowledge sacred and
never reveal (except directed by
his brother) this first sign and token of
God's full and final dispensation to
the human family.

He *meant* well. And,
he held his tongue for longer than you might
expect. But Samuel was just a boy
and, foreordained to labor as the first
of all the missionaries who would bear
his Brother's message, couldn't keep the good
news to himself indefinitely.

By
November, Joseph's bag was catless, and
the news reached Reverend Beeston just as he
had settled by the fireside for a dose
of Epiphanius before he put
the Sabbath Day to rest. The Widow Byrd,
that pious gossip, bustled in to share
The Revelation of Joe Smith, and he
received her message with the same keen thrill

that stirred the hearts of sailors on the whale-
ship *Essex*—in that very moment, on
the other side of this revolving globe,
astride the pulsing South Pacific—at
the cry of "There she blows!"

Old heresies
revived by an American farmer:
Who would have thought that Joseph Smith, because
he found our synod inhospitable,
should then imagine he was capable
of forming a proprietary church
and system of theology? Of course
there is no question of succeeding; Smith's
zeal will evaporate before it's crossed
the little walls of stone that walk the line
between his own fields and his neighbor's. How
does he expect to gather followers?
The man can hardly speak, and publishing
the terms of his perverted testament
will take a better grasp of grammar than
an unlearned farmer's conversation can
sustain in black and white. And how will—

But
the Reverend's reverie was broken up
by his renewed awareness of the Byrd's
chirping: ". . . so I told Phlyaros I thought
a boy his age might have a little—"

"Boy?
But I had thought—which is to say . . . the son?"
That he, a minor, should presume to know
God's will and arrogate authority
belonging to his betters so enraged
old Beeston that he preached on nothing but
submission to your elders for a year.
He proved that children are natural slaves,
unfit to rule themselves or others, in
a hundred ways: with sermons on the Fifth
Commandment and the proper worship of
Jehovah; on the load of Isaac and

his binding; on the Savior's thirty-year
apprenticeship to Joseph; and on Paul's
confession that, as Saul, he thought and spoke
as children do—until a call to the
Apostleship forced him to put aside
his puerile ways.

Lectured and taunted by
the people of Palmyra, Joseph turned
again to God in prayer—but nothing came.
No unexpected flash of insight with
the Spirit's sweet confirming peace; no still
small voice to whisper words of counsel and
command; no smoking lamp or dewy fleece
to signify the will of Father and
his Firstborn. Whether swayed by Beeston's proofs
against the leadership of anyone
still shy of his majority; or slow
to answer after prior messages
were lightly treated; or reluctant to
condemn the boy with dictates he could not
be counted on to keep—whatever his
pure purpose, God was silent.

Joseph, to
be fair, was hardly knocking at the door
of heaven urgently enough to rouse
its porter. Like a pilgrim in pursuit
of fields more free and fertile, who arrives,
surprised, beside an unknown sea between
himself and his next waypoint, then forgets
his journey while enjoying all that beach
living can offer, Joseph wallowed. He
indulged in angst and thoughts of martyrdom.
He hunted treasure with his father, and
he dreamed of kissing Leah Sullivan.
He was a teenage boy who loved a joke
and farted more than his fair share. So too,
in truth, did Zechariah: prophets share
the weaknesses of human nature and
endure an adolescence also.

On
September twenty-first, three years now past
since he saw God's wet footprint in the sand,
headed for water, Joseph was impressed
into the service of his King. That night,
as Joseph tossed and turned in search of sleep,
he felt the stirrings of a dream that had,
in evenings past, disturbed his peace. He roused
himself to kneel beside the bed and prayed
for unadulterated rest, but light—
at first a solitary pinprick, like
a firefly come auditioning for work
as Joseph's personal pole star; and then,
the prick expanded, took on human shape
and came like lightning to his bedside, with
a searing brilliance which forbade the dark—
light banished thoughts of sleep from Joseph's brain.
This personage of midnight sun, whose light
had failed (the greatest miracle of all,
as Joseph joked in later days) to wake
his siblings, stood three inches off the ground
with nothing but a loose white robe between
his nakedness and chill autumnal air.

Without regard for placing words aright,
the angel shared his errand: "Joseph, my
name is Moroni. God has work for you
to do, and he has sent me here to give
you revelations and commandments not
a few. Close by, deposited within
an earthen bank, are plates of gold on which
a partial history is written of
this continent's first peoples and their deeds
and origins, including a report
of Jesus Christ: his ministry beyond
the grave to these, the other sheep he spoke
of, and the fullness of his gospel. With
the book are two interpreters—stones set
in silver bows athwart a breastplate—called
Urim and Thummim. You must use the stones
to translate this account and to invest
its ancient principles with currency,

sent forth to all the world in paper. As
it circulates throughout the earth, your name
shall be pronounced in every language; blessed
and cursed by every nation; spoken by
all peoples.

"Behold, I the Lord will send
my messenger, and he prepares the way
before me, and the Lord you seek shall come
suddenly, to a temple you shall build,
in swift fulfillment of my covenant.
Today this scripture is accomplished in
your sight." Moroni's message, after that, came through
in fits and snatches: "*. . . leave them neither root*
nor branch . . . and turn the hearts of children to
their father . . . Jesse, and a Branch shall grow
from out his roots; and . . ." Like an analog
radio signal interrupted by
the canyonlands that human trains of thought
traverse, all serpentine, the angel's words
negotiated the topography
of Joseph's brain and found an audience
with only intermittent clarity.

And then, before he'd even understood
the interview was over, Joseph saw
a conduit to heaven open, and
Moroni disappeared, relinquishing
the room again to tarry blackness. Yet
the subtleties of night-sight he'd accrued
before the angel's visit still remained.
No dilatory reacquaintance with
the dark; his vision seemed to comprehend
a broader portion of the spectrum now,
as though the primary effect of this
encounter was to render him a prism—
refracting the invisible but all-
pervading covenantal light of Christ
into observable new frequencies.

In bed, as he was lying, musing on
the singularity of fortune and
the golden book that would, apparently,

make his, another point of light, in size
and contour like a needle's eye, caught his,
and then that body full of glory stood
again beside him. Other angels might
have gone off book and bollocksed up the whole
production, as when Milton's Raphael
suborned the garden, but Moroni spoke
his lines verbatim, giving word-for-word
the same exact performance: "Joseph, I,
Moroni, have been sent by God to teach
you of the work he has prepared for you . . ."

This time, familiar with the substance of
his visitor's instructions, Joseph turned
aside his thoughts of gold just long enough
to hear the prophecies that had escaped
him earlier. And new ones too: the youth's
attention authorized the angel to
provide additional perspective on
the coming judgments—famine, pestilence,
and sword—that would afflict the wicked of
this generation. Overwhelmed by thoughts
of the apocalypse, he almost missed
the end of revelation, as the Bright
and Morning Star received Moroni to
himself, and Joseph was returned to night.

But only for the space of half an hour,
and then the veil of heaven was drawn back
a third time, so Moroni could repeat
his message yet again and add a word
of caution: "Satan will attempt your heart
and introduce your indigence as an
inducement to regard the golden plates
more for their monetary value than
their everlasting purpose in God's plan
for the salvation of his family.
This you must never do. The Lord will not
permit you to retrieve the record if
you go with any other motive than
the building of his kingdom."

Joseph, who
had been a mute throughout the night now found
his voice: "To sell the plates for money would
deny the very means by which I came
to know of their existence and secured
them for myself—for God, I mean, of course."
But since the angel had departed as
he spoke, these final words of protest found
no audience. Or so the youth assumed
until the crowing cock reminded him
of God's omniscience, omnipresence, and
forgiveness. And, his morning chores.

Worn out
and weary from the night's unrest—or lost
in mazy contemplation of his new
responsibilities—he stumbled through
the rituals of daybreak wrapt in fogs
figurative and gaseous, sweating at
the apron-edge of harmony. Aware
that Joseph wasn't working with the same
enthusiasm he habitually
exuded, Alvin urged his brother to
extend his sickle with some might, and reap,
before the sun could bleach
their grain from golden green to bone and cause
it, overripe, to drop. But Senior saw
his namesake stagger with the blade and sent
him home for Mother's doctoring. En route,
he stopped to pluck an apple, sat to eat,
and woke to find Moroni there before
him, standing in the air.

"Again?" he asked.
The angel gave his message for a fourth
time, nothing varying, until he'd run
iteratively through the whole, and then:
a new commandment.

"Joseph, go and tell
your father all that you have heard and seen."
With holy purpose and the energy

it gave him, Joseph searched out Alvin and
his father in the field, where he rehearsed
for them his new commission to retrieve
the book and publish its invaluable
account of Indian religion. They
accepted, without question, his report
of heaven's distillations, dewy-eyed
and joyful.

Each embraced the others, and
then Alvin, smiling, asked: "Well, brother, what
are you delaying for? Go get that book
and read whatever's written in it—I
expect that we can deal with this gold here
while you unearth a finer mill. Be quick
and run, before the angel figures out
he's picked a slow apprentice and revokes
your covenants!"

He raced off to obtain
the plates, first jogging home to fetch a sack
and tools, then heading for a local hill
Moroni called Cumorah. When he reached
the place appointed, Joseph levered up
a stone from off the sepulcher wherein
the word lay buried—like a golden seed
whose ancient roots had tapped the lifeblood of
a hemisphere, now poised to stem and branch
and blossom in the bistre, cream, and red
of Aaron's almond rod. But awe is not
sustainable in breathing beings; grown
familiar with the cache's contents, he
bent over, hoisted up the plates and the
interpreters, and gently placed them in
his burlap bag.

Then Joseph turned to go,
but looking back saw treasures with a past
and sacred purpose he could not begin
to guess—Mahonri's stony suns, the sword
of Laban, Zeezrom's onties—and had thoughts
of home and parents destitute despite

FIGURE 6. “A Boy Yet Unworthy.” Godwin.

unceasing toil. *Moroni never spoke*
of other riches, Joseph mused, and loosed
his grip upon the sack to stretch again
into the silent tomb. *Perhaps I can—*

He couldn't. When he woke, his molars ached,
and though he longed to bend his knees and flex
his throbbing fingers, he seemed paralyzed,
unable to direct his body—saw
the sack was empty; saw the stone lid back
atop its cairn; and realized he had lost
the plates.

Despair descended like a shroud,
engulfing him in shame, and Joseph longed
for death. What followed, though, caused him to ask
if he might be a corpse already, damned
to a Promethean eternity.
The forest's undertakers bubbled up
beneath him in a frenzy, like some dark
libation spued back up by earthy gods:
centipedes, spiders, earwigs, earthworms, ants,
and salamanders. As they swarmed around
and over him, the bite of mandibles
and pincers in increasingly discreet
and tender places drove him nearly to
distraction, and he saw—or thought he saw—
demonic faces flickering across
insectoid features, metamorphoses
too rapid and inconstant to discern
with confidence.

Just as an earwig reached
his nostrils, the assault was stopped: from no
place blessed reprieve came with Moroni's fifth
appearance. He commanded, "In the name
of Jesus Christ, depart." They left, and so
did his paralysis, but any joy
at this relief was dissipated by
the angel's stern demeanor. "You have sinned
and, for a moment, felt the buffetings
of Satan in the flesh, to teach you not

to trifle with the taint of darkness. Go,
and sin no more. The book is lost to you,
but you may yet repent and qualify
for service in the vineyard."

"Never? Am
I never to receive the plates? No terms
by which I might reclaim my privilege?"

"Come
again a year from now, with purer heart
and with the right companion. You shall be
instructed further and you may, if you
continue faithful, have the record four
years hence."

"But who should I bring with me? Who
is right before the Lord?"

"Bring Alvin." This
apparently concluded the exchange,
and Joseph made his way back home. Though he
was disappointed Joseph had returned
home empty-handed, Alvin felt a surge
of pride to know that God had chosen him
to play a part in bringing forth his word.
The brothers spoke of little else and soon
became inseparable, co-opting meals
and family devotionals with talk
of what Moroni had taught Joseph.

Too
abruptly, conversation ceased. Gall
of bitterness! The colic, calomel,
and then a coffin: Alvin's death came like
a thief at night, too sudden—terrible—
surprising—to resist or comprehend.
Malpractice, all agreed, but blaming the
physician was a barren comfort; hate
has yet to offer beauty for ashes.

The Reverend preached, in charity, from John,
"*I am the Resurrection and the Life,*"

but Joseph was not comforted and stayed
behind to share his doubts with Alvin: "How
could he have let you die? It isn't fair.
You said you'd come with me September, and
Moroni said I *have* to bring you with
me; what am I supposed to do, dig up
your bones and haul them to Cumorah?"

Here
he paused, expectantly, as though the witch
of Endor might, at any moment, raise
his brother from the turf to answer these
complaints. Of course, she didn't. Peace of mind,
like any other peace, is always free
but seldom cheap. So Joseph struggled on:
"Did I mishear? No. When he spoke, he spoke
in English, and his terms for taking up
the plates were unambiguous.

"Could he
have been mistaken? Angels are just men
made perfect; maybe his infallibility
is pending, still in progress. If
Moroni can't be trusted, though, what grounds
have I for seeking to retrieve the plates?
That way lies madness. Every gift is good
which comes from God, in whom there is no slant
or swerving: surely, then, his messenger
must also be beyond reproach.

"What else?
Perhaps I've sinned, offended God, and he
revoked my high commission. Have my sins
made you expendable in some divine
arithmetic? Remaindered? While I yet
remain to languish here below? Such thoughts
are insupportable. Take pity on
me, Lord: deliver me from grief and doubt!"

NEW COVENANTS
VOLUME 2

And because my words shall hiss forth—many of the Gentiles shall say: A Bible! A Bible! We have got a Bible, and there cannot be any more Bible.

—Nephi

With each new mind, a new secret of nature transpires; nor can the Bible be closed until the last great man is born.

—Emerson

IV

"But Joseph," Emma blurted from his side,
as they reclined, young lovers intertwined
in scandalous and innocent repose
along the riverbank, "we hadn't met
yet—when Moroni told you that to claim
the record you would have to bring the right
companion to Cumorah. Furthermore,
I can't see why an angel should regard
a man *more* worthy of his trust because
he managed to seduce an unabashed
but unwed maiden from her father's home
with talk of gold."

"Unwed? But I had thought—
which is to say, the question presupposed
that we would . . ." Rudderless, adrift in new,
uncharted waters, Joseph searched for firm
ground. In the upward curve of Emma's lips,
which bent to an inverted rainbow, as
a sign that she would no more give him cause
for doubt as to the singularity
and strength of her affections, Joseph found
his heading—and his tongue. Like some
pre-modern pilot sent a sextant, he
sailed onward, more assuredly, and sought
to know that nothing had been lost in his
translation of her silence: "Will you help
me liberate the plates and wrestle with
an angel? Be my wife, and come away

FIGURE 7. “The Prophet’s Companion.” Godwin.

with me before your father makes me swear
to seven years of servitude as bride
price for your hand."

"And if he were to give
you Tryael in my stead? What then? Could you
discern between two sisters in the dark?
Did Jacob even care whose waist he held
that night?"

"Not fair! Not fair," laughed Joseph, "when
his father, Isaac, was himself half-blind.
Remember how he couldn't tell which son
was which, and Esau lost the birthright? Two
stories, the same distressing end to each.
And why? Because far-sighted men, whose eyes
habitually scan the heavens, trained
to see, across the centuries, the rise
and fall of nations, gradually lose
their sense of what's important, in the here
and now, to those whose field of vision is
more circumspect. At Jacob's feet, perhaps,
some blame I grant—"

"You grant me, hedgehog? Peace!
You court like Richard Crookback making love
to Lady Anne. Was ever woman wooed
with talk of buried, ancient histories?
Was ever woman won? I'll have you; but
you will not keep me long unless you take
a more myopic view than Abraham
and his successors. Just remember how,
when Sarah died, her husband heard the news
from foreigners because he couldn't see
his error in absconding with the dawn
to sacrifice her son. If ever I
should catch you using spectacles to read
or write, that will be sign enough of your
far-sightedness to send me off in search
of some more biddable man. Come, kiss me, now,
and no more talk of golden plates. For where
thou goest, I will go; where diggest, I

will dig. Thy angels be my angels; and
thy God, my God."

Four lips, two souls, but one
desire; *e pluribus unum*, and this
reduction into unity no less
a miracle than multiplying loaves
and fishes. *That they may be one*, he prayed,
and though he answers our petitions for
relief each day, so seldom do we grant
his singular request that till the great
millennial day, a sacramental kiss
is all the earnest he receives some years.
Smith died a little death when Emma's lips
had paid in full; the youth who came to court
her nevermore arose.

The winter of
his discontent made glorious summer by
her coy assent, New York's adopted son
marveled to see himself through Emma's eyes,
a prophet like the patriarchs of old,
and felt himself new-made by love, reborn
and weaned from all his doubts. *So that was what*
Moroni meant, thought Joseph later, when
spontaneous emotion's overflow
was recollected in tranquility.
His talk of bringing the appropriate
companion wasn't meant to help me find
another but to help me find myself,
in being seen and heard and known by one
who loves me. Like an echo of the man
he'd been before their rendezvous, a more
resonant version of the Joseph who proposed,
attuned to fundamental frequencies,
he basked beneath unseasonably strong
mid-winter sunbeams, consonant with both
the Lehi Valley's steadfast hillslopes and
the Susquehanna's constant flow.

They wed
immediately. Emma knew that her

decision would be met with tears and worse
if Joseph traveled back to Harmony
and asked her father's blessing, so they made
the journey to the magistrate's alone.
No friends or family to cheer them on
and strew their path with flowers, but a grin
of recognition broke across the Squire's
congenial features when he opened up
the door.

"Glass-looker!" he exclaimed. "Appears
you found your treasure after all."

"Her price
surpasses that of rubies," Joseph laughed,
"and precious stones are rare enough around
these parts, as I know well."

"I take it that
you've had no fortune, then, divining where
they buried all those Spanish dollars?"

"No,
your Honor," Emma interjected. "My
husband, if you will make him so, has not
unearthed a single piece of silver and
no longer digs for money."

"But of course
not—not with you to fill his looking glass.
Come in! Come in, and I will name you man
and wife." Consent was sought, consent received,
and through the alchemy of law, they twain
became one flesh, a corporate person with
shared rights and obligations. Marriage made
no visible impression on the mien
of either party, yet they felt themselves
transfigured by the covert power of
that primal institution. Striding from
the Squire's estate, the world was all before
them, yet their domestic tranquility
was pending some more perfect union's form,
to guide their wandering steps.

With nothing but
the clothes upon her back, Emma endured
the trip to Manchester, where wedded bliss
was tempered by the stress of living cheek-
by-jowl with Joseph's parents. Far from home;
no female confidante to empathize
with wifely joys and strains; no room to call
her own, much less the means to furnish it,
she shouldered the connubial yoke.

"Perhaps,"
her husband ventured, "if you wrote to ask
your father, he would send your furniture
and clothing. When the weather turns, your cows
could come as well."

"Whose cows?" she asked.

"Your cows."

"Not mine. Zach Tarbill, with a penstroke, struck
me from the legal record, stripped me of
my household stuff, my field, my barn, my horse,
my ox, my ass, my anything."

"They still
are yours, regardless. I would never take
pecuniary action of my own
accord, without consulting you."

"I know,
my love, but that's the problem: you can act,
and I cannot. The most that I can hope
for is a husband who will listen."

"Let
us go to law, then, and request the courts
acknowledge you my deputy. Such things
have been before."

"And after all of that
expense of time and money, will the cows
be mine? A contract is no contract if
it alters when it alteration finds,

and individual adaptation is
inadequate as a solution for
systemic ills. Just promise that, when God
asks you to form a new society,
you will remember us—the ladies—too."

He bowed his head and promised her, "Yes."

"Thank
you," Emma answered. "That will do for now,
until Moroni comes to give the book
into your custody. But afterwards,
could we, perhaps, return to Harmony?
By then my father should be ready to
forgive me for eloping and to greet
you as his son-in-law."

This prophecy
bore fruit before the day of harvest had
arrived. In June a letter came, addressed
to Mrs. Emma Smith, from Isaac Hale,
inviting her—and, more importantly,
her husband—back to Pennsylvania and
her father's homestead. They accepted this
armistice as the miracle it was
and worked as though they had no knowledge of
the one to come.

But others knew. They watched
and waited for September twenty-first
to pass; for Joseph to unearth the gold;
for time and space to steal it. Willard Chase
and old Sam Lawrence both believed themselves
entitled to a share of anything
discovered by their former partner—Chase
because he'd found the seerstone Joseph used
for scrying; Lawrence due to Joseph's poor
decision two years prior, when he'd tried
to bring the older man in Alvin's stead,
to get the record. Friends came too, and each
was eager to contribute. Just as well,
for Joseph realized, as the witching hour

arrived, that he would soon have fifty pounds
of sacred relics in a sack, with no
conveyance but his own appendages.
With Emma's feet in mind, he borrowed horse
and wagon (stole? semantics) for the trip
from Joseph Knight, who'd come to witness the
fulfillment of Moroni's promise but
was sleeping when they left, at midnight.

"You
want me to what?" she asked.

"To wait," said Joseph for
the second time, descending from his seat
atop the wagon. "I need you to wait
below while I climb up the hill and fetch
the plates."

"But why? Why can't I come and meet
the angel and keep watch for you? Why let
Sam Lawrence mount the hill but not your wife?"

"When Lawrence came, I couldn't even find
the stone that marks the record's hiding place.
And if I fail again, what then? I fear
that bringing you will seem presumptuous
and lead to condemnation. Please?"

Although
she had to bite her lip to stop herself
from mentioning that perfect love casts out
all fear, Emma agreed and nodded: "Yes."
He strode away for God and glory; she
kept questions for her company. *What good*
can I accomplish sitting here while he
retrieves an ancient book of scripture? Why
does he need me *for a companion if*
I can't assist him in his labors? Why
would he need anyone? A helpmeet who
can't help or even meet with those who helm
the work is hardly worthy of the name.
But is it true that I can't help? Or has

my husband substituted prejudice
against my sex for heavenly decree?
If Lawrence or his brother Alvin had
been chosen, neither would have stayed behind.
But maybe that's why Joseph needed me
instead, a consort who can share his task
without usurping it and see him as
a prophet, not a younger brother. Then
frustration, fear, and loneliness returned,
and Emma found herself revisiting
the questions she began with, picking at
a knot whose ravelings resisted all
attempts to tease out human agency
from foreordained events.

They also serve
who only stand and wait, and Emma stopped
her ears with prayer against the siren song
of martyrdom, her night a hymn to praise
the better fortitude of patience and
heroic meekness. She kept watch until
the dawn, as Lucy would, and Joseph spied
her through the trees, before his own approach
was noticed. She was beautiful, he saw
anew, despite—because of—her unkempt
appearance. Contemplation lent her eyes
the tincture of eternity and drew
her lips into a secret smiling, framed
by wanton ringlets bouncy with surprise,
black wires unspooling and recoiling to
the distant beat of silent drums, untamed,
against the tawny dun of Emma's cheeks.

Before he could announce his presence, she
perceived him near and saw the absence in
his arms. With horror, Emma raised her hands
to mutely query: Had he lost the plates?

But Joseph's grin broke wide across his face
in reassurance: "All is well—no, ten
times better." With the record, he explained,
the angel left an urgent warning, that

unscrupulous associates would try
to steal the book, "And so I hollowed out
a log where they'll be safe until I can
secure them from the public view. But these
I kept, and they are marvelous!" He reached
into his pocket and withdrew a silk
handkerchief knotted in a bundle. As
his overeager fingers fumbled with
the fabric, Joseph gushed, "They're better than
the stone I found in Willard's well. He called
them *selah*. Maybe *stela*?" (*Tsohar*.) "I
can see the truth of anything, of things
to come and secret things and mysteries.
Moroni said that I should use them to
interpret and that he had done the same,
translating records of the earliest
inhabitants of the Americas."

"Before the Indians?"

"Before the fall
of Babel's tower—there were some, he said,
who left to keep their language perfect, and
Moroni's people found a history
of their migration to this hemisphere,
the book of Eber, and it documents
their downfall as a nation—civil wars,
uncivilly conducted; famine; drought;
and plague, until the kindling breath of God
withdrew. And with the history, they left
the means to translate what was written."

From
within the handkerchief he drew a pair
of prehistoric pince-nez, reading stones
encircled by a silver band which wound
around itself, between the stones, into
a supinated figure eight. The stones
themselves were oddly uniform, as if
they had been cast, like molten glass, in molds,
or if—a single egg disgorging two
great lizards that, on their majority,

fell side-by-side into the deep, until,
subducted and digested by the earth,
their hearts compressed into zirconia—
twin stones had been deposited beneath
a vein of magma and released with one
stroke of a miner's pickaxe. Even where
the stones were smudged by Joseph's fingers, she
could see the whorls and ridges marring her
reflection were aligned. Reflexively,
she drew the handkerchief across each face,
but burnishing could no more wipe away
that imprint than a boll of cotton staunch
the broad Missouri's flow and swab it dry.

Not Joseph's finger, Emma realized. Whose
and how and therefore what were questions that
would have to wait. Her husband had begun
to speak of getting back and how he hoped
to purchase peace of mind: a chest in which
to keep the record safe from cupid eyes
and roving hands. The need for such a thing
became apparent sooner than they feared
it would.

Before the prophet could afford
to buy a chest; before he'd even struck
the water he was digging for, to put
some money in his purse, his father told
him of an organized attempt to find
the place where he had laid the book to rest:
"As I came home on the Vienna Road,
halfway, I thought I heard a voice direct
me to the Lawrences', but when I turned
and saw that there was no one near, assumed
I had imagined it. No matter, so
I started on my way again until
a messenger descended from the skies
and stopped me short."

"An angel?" Joseph asked
his namesake.

"No, a bird."

"Was it a dove?"

"A pigeon; no."

"I would have thought, if God
intended to communicate his will
through feathered things, that he would send a dove,
the way he spoke to Noah."

"No; a dove
was sent," said Emma, "but the Lord was not
the one who bade it fly. Perhaps if men
were willing to accept his word without so much
attention to the form of those who brought
it, we would see his hand in kestrels, jays,
and magpies wimpling morning skies—our hearts
stirred for a bird regardless of its guise.
Elijah might have starved if he had spurned
the raven's sooty wing because it was
unclean according to the law. But we
digress. Please tell us, Father Smith, how you
could see that this was more than a surprise
encounter with the bird."

"Well, like I said,
just past the stand of trees that marks the turn-
off for Old Sam's, I heard a voice, but when
I turned around to keep on walking, there
it was, eye level, hovering, its wings
beating me back. As I retreated, it
descended, but if I advanced it rose
again, to bar my path. Who dances with
a pigeon? Still, since she seemed bound to have
me for a partner, I obliged and stepped
it lively: ten, nineteen, seventy-eight
steps back before that bird abandoned our
duet and glided to the ground. With cocked
head and a burbled invitation, she
requested that I follow as she hopped
along the track to Sam's place. I declined
at first, but when she took my trousers in

her beak and started tugging, I gave up
kicking against the pricks, accepting that
this tame wild pigeon was a messenger
from heaven.

"What I found at Lawrence's
removed all doubt on that score: he and twelve
men of unsavory appearance, whose
affinity for drink was manifest
in oaths and imprecations shocking to
the ear, were taking supper off a log
he'd sawn in half. They greeted me with jeers
and boasts that by this time tomorrow they
would have the record. When I scoffed and asked
how they would find the gold without a map
or guide, Willard and Abel Chase called out
in unison, "Hey Sal!" and she appeared
behind them, like a spirit summoned to
the threshold of another world, and in
her hand that looking-glass you taught her how
to use. Then, stepping from Sam's cabin door
and lifting up her glass, she turned the day's
last light a sickly green and spoke: 'You know
what I can do with this, and so does Joe.
We mean to have that gold, and you can tell
him that I've seen the birch he hollowed out
to hide it in. A dozen pairs of eyes
should be enough to find a single log
by moonlight. Right, my boys?' I didn't wait
for their huzzahs but turned and ran for home,
stiff leg and all. Could she be bluffing?"

"No."

"How long can we afford to dither, then
in conversation? Say the word, my son,
and I can rouse a band to rival Sam's."

The son was silent, briefly, then, "All life
is precious in the sight of God, and if
I counter force with force there will be blood—
perhaps a body—laid to my account.

Better that I should perish than be held
responsible for even one man's death,
however wicked. No—I go alone,
and if I die, the Lord will bring about
his righteous purposes through someone else."
A kiss for Emma, and he left to fetch
the record.

Not until he held it in
his hands did Joseph realize he'd not brought
a sack with which to carry home the plates
and shield his neighbors from temptation. Off
his back, a tug, a twist, and several knots
secured his shirt around the golden book.
He stood and slung the weighted cloth across
his naked shoulder just in time to hear
a rifle cocking. Providentially,
for Joseph—or, perhaps, predictably,
depending on your faith in forecasts made
by actuaries on the likelihood
of accidents involving alcohol
and firearms—his assailant's gun misfired.
The howling blasphemies suggested Sam
and Sally's dozen was eleven now,
but Joseph took no comfort in the odds
against him dropping some. He ran for home,
the only place and people he felt sure
had not the least desire to honor him
with martyrdom.

Like Jacob, going back
to Canaan, Joseph made for home, and like
the patriarch, he had to wrestle for
the privilege of arriving there alive.
Careening shirtless through the forest, he
considered that he might be dreaming, or
somnambulating, but the body that
came crashing into his laid Joseph's head
to rest on stony pillows and convinced
him otherwise. They grappled in the dust,
two shadows straining; clenching; trembling with

exertion. Neither could prevail until,
when Joseph felt the man release his grip
to scrabble for a rock, which broke the earth
where Joseph's head had been a beat before,
the prophet seized one arm with two and wrenched
it backwards, counter-clockwise, out of joint.

No time to set it right, with ten more men
still looking for him. Running home, the word
of God clutched safely to his breast, pursued
by Sam and Sally's tribe, he recognized
the voice that raged behind him: "Curse you, Joe!
Let come what may—I'll be revenged of you
for this!" The words were Abel's, but his deeds
belonged to Cain, and no one contemplates
revenge more constantly than those who know
themselves the perpetrators of a wrong
they fear can never be forgiven, though
the one unpardonable crime is to
revenge. How could a sailor, anchored to
some seeming island, who awoke to find
it was Leviathan, adrift, and took
revenge with kicks—who had his leg bit off
and swore an oath to hunt the guilty brute
with unrelenting hatred, though it cost
himself and all his crew their lives, in an
expanding, all-consuming spiral of
reprisal, till the world was toothless, blind,
and left adrift—be pardoned? Who could weep
for such a one this side of Eden? Who
could tell him *timshel*? Taking vengeance is
a categorical rejection of
the Savior's power to forgive and his
investiture as Judge. By setting up
ourselves in place of God, declaring war
against the Prince of Peace, we nurture sins
whose penalty must be expulsion: death.

But Joseph, fleeing for his life, had not
the breath to muse upon such matters. As
a boy the prophet needed surgery

FIGURE 8. “Joseph’s Flight.” Godwin.

to save his leg from amputation, and
he still walked haltingly; however, in
this hour of need his limp became a lope,
outstripping all who chased behind him. Does
it seem incredible that Joseph, with
a gimpy leg and fifty pounds athwart
his back, could win a footrace? Hector ran
like Joseph once, before the wrath of fleet
Achilles, not for glory or a prize
but for his very life, a good man whose
survival was decided by divine
decree. If it was *your* life on the line,
dear reader, *your* salvation in the sack,
how fast could *your* feet fly? How many miles
until you would be willing to lay down
and die? Believe; although it seems a deed
of myth or legend, Joseph fought the good
fight, ran the race, and came off conqueror
in both—and whether by adrenaline
or grace, the means is less important than
the outcome.

Stumbling breathless, bloody, bruised
into his brother's waiting arms, as though
he were a self-emancipated slave
arriving on the northern bank of the
Ohio, Joseph felt that he was at
the end of all his troubles. So he was,
perhaps, though not the end for which he hoped;
Ohio isn't Canada. But the
theatrical, Ohio seasons of
his life—the mummies and the bank collapse;
the private army mustered, marched across
the country, and dismissed before a drop
of blood was shed; and the erection of
a temple whose espousals are the main
reason the world has people in it—all
was yet futurity. In Hyrum's arms
the prophet briefly felt a boy again,
when wine and other drugs were powerless
to ease his aching leg, and only clutched

to Hyrum's breast, in endless circuits of
the sickroom, could he find relief. Not yet
the elder, though he would be soon, and yet
unwilling to be carried this time, like
the little brother he had always been—
despite the fact that he could hardly stand,
Joseph declined fraternal aid and limped
beside him to the house.

Confusion reigned
within. Had he been injured? What about
the record? Who attacked him? Did he think
the dangers passed, or should they set a watch?
He answered as he could but struggled with
the silent queries posed by every pair
of eyes that lingered on the bundle in
his lap. When Abraham, on Ishmael's
behalf, requested an expansion of
the covenant, no reason for the Lord's
refusal was revealed; and when he sought
consent to share his carnal knowledge of
the golden plates, no rationale for their
exclusion answered Joseph's question: *Why?*
Why not affirm their faith by sight? The foot
of one whose hand had held the word of God—
not Wycliffe's words or those of James and all
the translators but his, the same as if
they'd touched the stony tables Moses brought
down Sinai's switchbacks—surely such a foot
could never slide from off the Rock of our
Salvation. I can understand why Sam
and Sally couldn't be allowed to see
the record, casting pearls before the swine.
But why not Emma or my parents? All
my family and friends have gathered. If
it has to be concealed from those I love
and live with, where will I find safety, space,
and time to delve the record's meaning for
myself? Its size and shape are visible
to all, despite my linen shirttails, and
the effort needed just to shift so small

a parcel one arm to the other should
be evidence enough the plates are made
of gold. Or lead; their color can't be seen.
Is that what I conceal, removing all
that glisters from the sight of those who might
be tempted?

PEACE AND PATIENCE: MANY HERE
SHALL SEE THE RECORD, IN MINE OWN DUE TIME.

Inaudibly, the words resounded through
his mind, as though thoughts higher than his own,
in perfect diapason, tuned the voice
of his subconscious intellect to its
most fundamental frequency. He knew
that God had spoken. Joseph knew, and told
those present what he'd learned.

In retrospect,
the prophet recognized that this was a
mistake, that revelation is like salt:
a curative whose savor can become
a scourge if trodden into fertile ground
and not massaged into a votive flank.
With good intentions, those who heard him speak
translated Joseph's declaration for
their friends and neighbors, publishing good news,

". . . that all who had or would support him through
this present trial . . ."

". . . soon, I'm sure he said
it would be soon . . ."

". . . could turn its pages for
ourselves!"

The curious arrived with cash,
the idle with a jug; the learned came
with expertise, the clergy with reproach.
Such offerings were spurned, like Cain's, with calm
indifference, but to the seekers, with
their mustard seeds, the prophet had respect

and spoke of harvests yet to be. If none
but these had kept his family from their
autumnal labors, Joseph might have stayed.
His old compatriots, however, still
believed themselves entitled to the plates
and grew more brazen in their efforts to
secure them. Gangs of ten or twelve would raid
a home, a barn, a workshop, anywhere
that Sally glimpsed the gold, and ransack from
the floorboards to the furnishings. As yet
the record hadn't been discovered, but
the status quo was unsustainable,
so Joseph wrote to Emma's father and
accepted Isaac's invitation back
to Harmony.

He drew the gold from its
obscurement in a bed of flax, too young
to know to count the cost beforehand (not
that Joseph Murdock was a name he would
have recognized in any case), although
the price of gold from flax has always been
a son: your only son. But debts are paid
tomorrow, by our future selves; for that
moment, it was enough that he'd received
and kept the covenant. He kept it in
a cask of beans for the duration of
their journey back to Pennsylvania, where
the prophet sought reprieve from prying eyes
and fingers. No such luck—when Isaac heard
his no-good, treasure-digging son-in-law
had found a cache at last, his bosom swelled
with generosity and even an
apology for Joseph; but, when he
was told the gold was holy and the word
of God, as if from Sinai, by divine
decree to be withheld from human view,
like Moses' face behind the veil; in short,
when he had realized that this charlatan
who stole his daughter now proposed to keep
her in a state of penury instead

of using what the Lord had given to
provide for those of his own household, he
laid down an ultimatum:

"Either you
show us this golden Bible here and now
or we no longer have a daughter by
the name of Smith." Their time in Harmony
seemed at an end before it had begun.

However, happily for Emma and
her groom, the other half of Isaac's *we*
felt disinclined to acquiesce in this
decision to disown her child, and said
so: "And if *you* show *our* sweet daughter, in
her delicate condition, to the door,
then I'll no longer have a husband by
the name of Hale." Just like her namesake, this
Elizabeth announced a birth and found
her husband dumbstruck; she gave shelter to
the couple, persecuted for their talk
of angels, waiting for the days of their
delivery to be accomplished. So
it was, and so it had been written. Great
with expectations for the year to come,
the Smiths could welcome eighteen twenty-eight
in peace and safety, thanks to her.

Before
they left New York, an older neighbor, who
was there the night that Joseph carried home
the record, learned of their departure and
prevailed upon the prophet to accept
a gift of fifty dollars. With this help
from Martin Harris, they made do until
the house that Emma's brother built was theirs
and Joseph found employment in the fields,
transmuting nature's early green to gold.
But how to get the golden into black
and white without debasing all that made
it precious? How to reproduce the truths
and beauties of a book he couldn't read?

A lack of privacy and threats of theft
prevented Joseph, in New York and while
he lived in Isaac's home, from handling and
examining the plates, but now that he
and Emma were emancipated from
parental supervision, nothing came
before his duty to decipher and
disseminate God's word.

Moroni had
already come—again—to chastise him:
"Exceeding great neglect," he'd said, and in
a voice that broke across the prophet's back
like thirty-nine. So now the record was
his daily bread, the only subject, as
it seemed to Emma, ever in his mouth.
Yet chewing with her on the problem of
translation hadn't made the characters
engraven on its golden pages less
inscrutable. Like hardtack, sent to sea
so indurate that sailors sometimes thought
they had been given stones instead of bread
and dipped it in the ocean so as not
to break their teeth, these scriptures needed to
be saturated in the prophet's tears
before his heart was soft enough to make
digestion possible. He copied out
the characters on scraps of paper that
he carried in his pockets, folding and
unfolding them as though the flight of crows
and jays, which wheeled above him as he worked,
reminded Joseph of the hieroglyphs
and might reveal to him their secrets, like
the cranes of shrewd Palamedes. Or when
he saw a rock face signed by finches for
a generation, scored by claw and beak,
perhaps he fancied, for a moment, he
had found a new Rosetta Stone and pulled
out his transcription of the record to
compare—as though an infinite array
of finches, on an endless plain of slate

for all eternity, could ever scratch
a sentence in reformed Egyptian, with
the English underneath. Whether because
he lacked a *templum* to facilitate
interpretation of the birdsign or
because his father's gift for augury
through animals could not accommodate
the quantity of revelation queued
and waiting for transmission, Joseph's first
attempts to render scripture into words
miscarried.

Next he tried the spectacles,
which worked impeccably for inquiries
on other matters. Was his family
in health? They were: the right-hand stone began
to glow, internal light refracting on
its surface, bending color into shape
and answering his question—he could see
his mother kneading dough, Don Carlos at
her side with pilfered not-yet-bread between
his fingertips, a secret smile upon
her lips. Was Widow Whitehead's southern field
on top of water? No: the left-hand stone
showed Joseph what was underground—a bed
of gravel running straight as rails and flat
enough to be a road. Her northern field?
Beside a sycamore which marked the line
between her land and Yeoman Coates, he saw
the water dancing up and running for
Lake Erie: yes, the right-hand stone had shown—
there was. However, queries on how best
to tie abstruse significations back
to sensible ideas and language met
with mixed results. Occasionally he
caught sight of faces and connected them
to characters, but character depends
on context; connotation; syntax. Names
drive inward an external self defined
by others; how could Joseph hope to learn
the names of people ripped untimely from

the social matrix that makes humans of
us all?

Persistently, these efforts to
restore a name and standing to the dead
were compromised by Joseph's struggles with
converting light to truth. "Imagine that
you're walking through an orchard," he explained
to Emma, "and a gust of wind blows off
ten thousand springtime petals, so that all
the air is filled with flowers flying past
your face. That's what it feels like when I look
directly at the record; I can't see
the branches for the blossoms or discern
an apple from a cherry tree, much less
produce the fruits that are supposed to prove
that I'm a prophet. Or, imagine that
you're lying underneath a waterfall
of light and trying to identify
each drop before it passes; part and whole
are indistinguishable!"

"Snow-blind," she
said thoughtfully. "Most of the time, when we
can't see, there's not enough light, but too much
will blind—like staring straight into the sun,
or when the snow becomes a mirror for
its rays, and just to look outside you have
to squint and blink. My father says that that's
how Matthew Talbot lost his sight. Our eyes
need light to see, but they must need some dark
as well. Perhaps the Lord made pupils black
because we need receptors for the dark
as well as light: Corinthians thirteen,
verse two, *For now we see as through a glass,
darkly*. Moroni's glasses—maybe you
could use them as you did the stone, inside
a hat." He doubted Emma's logic but
felt such desire for a solution to
his problem that he would have traveled from
Damascus to Samaria at her

suggestion, having sensed the spirit that
had prompted her proposal.

Still, the sight
of English words and phrases so surprised
that Joseph jerked his head up from the hat
before he'd had a chance to read them: "You
were right," he blurted out. "It works!" Unless
the too-white, naked body of the truth
is clothed in garments dark enough that its
refulgence dazzle gradually, all
the human race, like moths, would be consumed
in flame and every man be blind—so we
walk backwards into Father's tent, with bells
upon our feet, to seek the holiest
of holy places, where his presence is
the only source of light to penetrate
a night of our own making. Thus, success
for Joseph, by circuitous design,
or more straightforward hazard, came at last.

She grinned at the acknowledgment, to know
that she had been essential after all,
and with an eager curiosity
she asked: "What does it say?" He looked again
and recognized the characters that he
had copied from the record's first gold leaf
and puzzled over vainly. Underneath
each lexeme was the corresponding word
or phrase, in English reminiscent of
the King James Bible—whether because God
speaks in an idiom to which we are
accustomed or because he is, in fact,
an Englishman, the prophet neither knew
nor cared.

THE BOOK OF LEHI.

Being an
abridgment of the history prepared
by Lehi, after he obtained the plates
of brass from Laban, at the time of his

departure from Jerusalem. An account
of his afflictions in the wilderness
and how the Lord preserved his family
from hunger and rebellion as he led
them to the promised land. Together with
a record of their kings, until the reign
of King Mosiah.

As he read, the words
were scraped off what he thought was vellum, and
an unseen hand, with antiquated strokes,
refreshed the text. *Two coats of skins*, he thought,
and then a sheet for writing. How long till
the Lambskin is exhausted—gone? And whence
the vanished scripture?

Joseph shook his head
and asked that Emma scribe, then bowed a third
time to his work, and this is what she wrote:

V

And now, behold, I, Mormon, having been
commanded of the Lord that I should make
a record of the preservation of
this people from captivity and death,
according to the covenants which he
established with the fathers, from the time
of their departures from Jerusalem
until they ripened in iniquity—
for notwithstanding his longsuffering
and all his tender mercies, they despise
the Holy One of Israel and set
at naught their Savior, Jesus Christ, and I
have seen the end of this, their wickedness,
resisting unto blood, and it is one
continual revenge; wherefore I make
a record of my people's turn away
from him who brought them to the promised land.

I write to you, the remnants of the seed
of Jacob, and to you, who have become
the children of the covenant among
the Gentiles, disavowing every claim
of nation, kindred, tongue, and people. I
have seen your day and your rejection of
the record of the Jews, foretelling the
Messiah's coming; yea, ye persecute
the Jews and willfully misread their words,
which testify that Jesus is the Christ.

But I, who have no gift for writing, speak
with plainness to condemn the worship of
your own success and merits, rather than
the mercies of that Being who sustains
you breath to breath and day to day, and I
have prayed that you, despite the weakness of
my words, might read them with the Spirit's aid
and inspiration, so that you might see
and know as I do. Whoso reads this book
with steadfast purpose, nothing wavering,
will learn the truthfulness of all these things
which I have written and of many things
I leave unwritten. Ye possess my words
in plainness: if ye err, it is because
ye take no thought, to ask for what they have
been given you, and seek to justify
yourselves instead of seeking to receive
justification at his hand. But when
we meet again before the judgment bar
of Jesus Christ, then ye shall know that I
have spoken nothing unto you except
the Lord commanded me. Amen.

Now I
proceed with mine account of Lehi, whose
obedience preserved a nation. In
the final days of Hezekiah came
Isaiah to a man of Lachish with
a burden from the Lord: Thus saith thy
Deliverer, O Ramath. At this time
next year, thy wife shall bear a son, and he
shall be a reservoir of faithfulness;
a fount of righteousness thy son shall be,
when all the cisterns of Jerusalem
are cracked and dry. As Sampson's jawbone saved
three thousands of his brethren and the rod
of Moses saved three millions, so shall he
be made an instrument in rescuing
a multitude more numerous than grass;
posterity beyond the hairs of old
men's beards shall call him blessed. He must flee

before the wrath to come, for I, the Lord
of nations, will leave desolate the homes
of those who turn away from me to fill
with their own eloquence the mouths of gods
which cannot speak; nor silent idols, nor
petitions to the scepters which surround
my vineyard, can prevent its razing. In
a foreign land possessed by those to whom
your father Abraham is strange shall he
raise up an offshoot of my vineyard and
two mighty nations.

And it came to pass,
in the appointed time, that Rayael,
the wife of Ramath, was delivered of
a son and called him Lehi as the man
of God had said; and Ramath took the boy
to Egypt, that the prophet's words might be
fulfilled. Behold: now Lehi was the son
of Ramath, son of Bamael, who was
the son of Roshar, son of Joelhar,
who was the son of Jotham, youngest son
of Gideon. And now I must suppose
that ye, for whom this record is prepared,
remember to have read of Gideon,
how he went forth by night to overthrow,
with fear and trembling, all the altars of
his father, Joash, and, by stratagem,
his little band did cause their enemies
to flee before them. And his mother, who
taught Gideon to love and reason with
the Lord, was Tirzah, youngest daughter of
Zelophehad, the son of Hepher, son
of Gilead, the son of Machir, son
of that Manasseh born to Joseph, who
delivered Israel from famine in
the land of Egypt.

And it came to pass
that Lehi took to wife the daughter of
Anon, a priest of Khenmu from the east,

FIGURE 9. “The Babe Lehi in Egypt.” Godwin.

and Lehi called her Sara-yah, for she
had put away the false traditions of
her fathers. Now there was a famine in
the land, and Lehi took Sariah to
Jerusalem and dwelt there all his days
until the reign of Zedekiah, king
of Judah. And it came to pass that in
those days the Lord sent prophets to declare
repentance to the people, lest they be
destroyed, and Lehi was awakened to
a perfect knowledge of his sinful state
and, after he had left the temple, cried
unto the Lord:

Turn back my days to birth,
the nights to my conception, that my soul
might be refreshed! Like dew descending from
the heavens, like new wine unbottled, give
me moisture in old age and innocence
despite my years. Can babes lift up their arms
in vain? My hands shall reach the treetops and
my palms ascend above the eagles; yea,
my fingers shall surmount the stars and breach
the windows of thy mercy. Hear, O God,
the words of my mouth; hearken to my cries
and answer.

And it came to pass that as
he spake, a fiery pillar fell upon
the rock before him, and within the fire
two men and one, in form, the Son of God.
The other whispered, Lehi, hearken to
my Firstborn, and thou shalt, with all thy house,
be walled in jasper. When the Father's voice
had ended, Lehi lifted up his face
from off the ground and said, But who am I
that I should see the Man of Holiness,
mine eyes behold the Son of Man? Then came
the voice of the Redeemer, saying, I
am Jesus, the Anointed One, of whom
the prophets testified. My ears shall be
engraved, Isaiah wrote; my palms and wrists

be pierced, as Huldah witnessed; and my flesh
be lifted up and crucified, that all
the words of Zenock and of Neum might
be brought to pass. And all mankind shall be
delivered from the everlasting bands
of death and awful chains of hell, to be
encircled round about in loving arms
eternally. And thou art Lehi, and
upon this mouthpiece I will pour out grace
and teach thee all that thou shalt say. Behold,
thy sins have been forgiven thee, and I,
the Lord, remember them no more.

And now
when he had heard these words, he cried before
the Lord and said, O Jesus, look upon
my children also, in thy mercy: on
my firstborn Laman and on Lemuel,
on Nephi and on Sam, on Eden and
on Ruth; preserve them from the wrath to come
and make thy face to shine upon them. But
when Lehi lifted up his eyes, he saw
that Jesus had removed himself from thence;
nevertheless, he did not cease to pray
but cried again and vowed a vow, that if
his children and their mother might be spared
that he would give the tenth of all with which
the Lord had blessed him. As he spake, there came
into his mind a still, small voice which caused
his heart to burn; yea it did cause his limbs
to tremble, saying, Lehi, I will make
of thee another Israel, who crossed
the river Jordan and became two bands:
so thou shalt cross the waters, and thy seed
shall prosper in the land I have prepared
for thee. According to their diligence
and heed in keeping my commandments, I
will visit them, and they shall be my sheep
and I their Shepherd.

Now, when Lehi heard
these words, his faith in Jesus Christ began

to be unshaken, and he prayed again,
unwearyingly, for his kinsfolk in
Jerusalem: But peradventure, Lord,
the righteous number fifty; surely thou
wilt spare this city for the righteous' sake:
Shall not the Judge of all the earth do right?
And after many hours there came a voice
again to Lehi, saying: Who can stay
the wind, which bloweth where it listeth? None
can tell the source thereof or why it sent
the rains on just and unjust both. But man
is free to choose captivity and death
or liberty and life, and I cannot
constrain his agency lest I should cease
to be the Lord Omnipotent and all
my works of mercy be undone. They lean
upon a broken reed and pierce their palms;
they look for water in a cistern dry
and broken, troubling their own roofs, and have
inherited the wind. Nevertheless,
because of thy exceeding faith, I shall
provide a means whereby the innocent
which hearken to the warnings sent among
them, by the prophets and by visions, might
escape from bondage and the besom of
destruction. But the wicked, who reject
my counsels, shall be swept away in tears
and blood and blindness from this land, to wear
the golden chains of Babylon.

And now
a fullness of the words which Jesus spoke
cannot be written, but when Lehi heard
them, he began to tremble and to quake
and wonder what they meant and how these things
should be accomplished. And it came to pass
that after he received sufficient strength
to walk, that he departed for his house.
Now when Sariah saw that Lehi's face
did shine, she wondered and was troubled in
her mind, not knowing why he answered not

her salutation with a word but fell
upon his bed as though he had been dead.
And for the space of two and forty hours
Sariah fasted, calling on the Lord
and begging that her husband, who lay stiff
and stark and cool, should rise again. And now
it came to pass that he, on the third day,
awakened from this state to speak of all
that he had seen as he lay sleeping:

Like
his father Joseph, Lehi dreamed a dream
in which, behold: a Man descended from
the firmament in glory brighter than
the sun, and in his wake another twelve
came hasting, luminous as stars, that all
the nations of the earth might be condemned
or justified, according to the light
and knowledge they received. The first of those
sent forth to judge the world bestowed on me
a book and bade me read the burden of
Jerusalem:

Thus saith your High Priest
and King, whom ye revile, the Author whose
commandments ye have broken and whose name
ye trample on: Look fohr destruction. Ye
shall perish twice, in fire and ice, for I
have witnessed your abominations, wrought
in lust and hate, and cannot countenance
thy wickedness, but I will hide my face
from thee in thy distress and turn away
from thine extremity.

And now it came
to pass that when Sariah heard these things,
although she had not seen, yet she believed
and said, The Lord is on my side, and I
fear not, for what can man do unto me?
Hosanna, Lord, and prosper us in our
distress. And it was counted unto her
for righteousness.

And Lehi, having been
commanded to prepare a record of
the things which he had seen and heard, therefore
he sent his servant Olam to procure
a book wherein to write, according to
his recollection, all the words of God.
And now when Olam had returned, behold,
Sariah wrote the words which she had heard
her husband utter, nothing varying,
except to render all his speech in the
Egyptian characters which she had learned
while in the service of her father, not
knowing beforehand all the purposes
of God or how the smallness of these plates
constrains our speech. And it behooves us to
engrave our records in this mother tongue
because of its exceeding brevity.
Yea, notwithstanding the obscurity
of this, our language, and the awkwardness
of writing, I rejoice to have the means
wherewith to say the smallest part of all
I feel concerning Jesus Christ, for I
have seen his face and heard him pray, that we
might all be one, in him, as he is one
in spirit with the Father. Who can say
too much of Christ and of his righteousness?
Yea, who can glory overmuch in his
redeeming love? Behold, the Son of God
was crucified, that he might loose all men
from bondage and the pains of hell, and have
we not great reason to rejoice? If he
had carried Israel from Egypt but
abandoned us before the sea of reeds,
it would have been enough; if he had brought
us through the wilderness but suffered us
to be destroyed at Jericho, it would
have been enough; if he had dwelt among
us in Jerusalem but withheld dreams
from Father Lehi, warning of the wrath
to come, it would have been enough. But he
hath also given us this promised land,

and he doth prosper those who put their trust
in him. Yea, blessed be the Most High God,
because of his great mercies.

And now, I,
Mormon, return to making mine account
of Lehi, who, when he told all the truth
concerning Judah's being rent aslant
by Babylon, the people sought to take
away his life. Behold, and now it came
to pass, the Lord spake unto Lehi in
a night vision, commanding him to leave
behind the land of his inheritance,
his gold and silver and his precious things,
and to depart into the wilderness
with nothing save his family: and this
to the fulfilling of his covenant,
that they might be delivered. And it came
to pass that Lehi was obedient
and called his servant Olam, that he might
go free, and Olam's wife as well, and take
from Lehi's store sufficient for their needs.
But Olam spake unto his master, and
he said: Behold, I know this city of
my father David must be punished for
its deeds, and I believe in all thy words
concerning its destruction. Wherefore, leave
me not to perish here but suffer me
to go with thee into the wilderness,
and I will be thy slave forever.

Now,
when Olam made an end of speaking, he
brought Lehi to the doorpost of his house
and with a nail requested that he be
made fast to Lehi and Sariah through
the blood of the Lamb. But behold, the Lord
had hitherto instructed Lehi that
the land of promise, whither he was bound,
must be a land of liberty, and that
no manner of captivity should be
imposed on its inhabitants, or those

who place their brethren into bondage must
surely be struck from off its face when they
are ripened in iniquity. And for
this cause did Lehi gainsay Olam's prayer
and would not bore his ear. Nevertheless,
he spake again to Olam on this wise
and answered him: The Lord hath said that I
should take none other people with me on
this journey save it be my family;
and neither should I carry servants with
me, for the Lord delighteth not in bond
and free, in rich and poor, but would that all
men should be equal. Therefore, if ye would
that I should take you with me to this land
of promise, let us go as brothers. And
now after he had spoken, Lehi fell
upon his face and bowed unto the ground
three times; and then they kissed each other, and
they wept, together.

And it came to pass
that Lehi loaded camels with his tents
and with provisions and departed for
the wilderness. And for the space of three
days Lehi traveled with his family
until, behold, he pitched his tent beside
the sea and built an altar and gave thanks
for his safe passage from Jerusalem.
But two of Lehi's sons complained and would
that he should give them all that portion of
his goods which fell to them, dividing up
his living; saying that Jerusalem
should no more be destroyed than Babylon
itself—not knowing what the Lord had said
concerning this—and that the denizens
of that far country would have bread enough
to spare long after they had perished in
the wilderness with hunger; saying that
because of foolish dreams they languished in
a lone and dreary desert where they might
be torn apart by savage animals

or tortured by the bands of lawless men
who terrorized inhabitants of all
the country round about Jerusalem;
and saying that their father was a vain
and foolish man who thought to make himself
a prophet for the honor of the world
and who confided overmuch in dreams
of an uncertain origin. But he
reproved them sharply and recalled to their
remembrance all the words of Habakkuk
and Jeremiah, who had spoken of
the woe to come, for in the mouths of two
or three the Lord establisheth his truth,
and sendeth other witnesses; thus, we
are left without excuse. And he refused
their importunity, but spoke to them
with gentleness and meekness and with love
unfeigned; thus Lehi, by persuasion and
longsuffering, prevailed with Laman and
with Lemuel, and they, at length, did come
unto themselves, repenting of their sins.

But Nephi hearkened to his father, and
the Lord did visit him with further light
and knowledge; for this reason Lehi and
Sariah did rejoice in Nephi and
in Sam, another Nephi; and in Ruth
and Eden, for their faithfulness; but more
especially did they delight to see
that Lemuel and Laman had put off
the galling chains of pride, acknowledging
themselves unprofitable servants and
unequal to the measure of the gift
of God's equality.

And now it came
to pass that Lehi did rehearse unto
the Lord in prayer the words of Lemuel
and Laman, touching the destruction of
Jerusalem and their petition to
return and garner their inheritance.

And now in answer to his cries, the Lord
did visit Lehi in the night, and when
the morning came, he roused his eldest sons
and said, Awake, O Laman, and arise,
O Lemuel! and hear the merciful
bequest of your Almighty King: Behold,
I dreamed a dream in which methought I saw
a man in purple robes, and on his head
a crown: he made a proclamation, Who
among you worshippeth the Lord? Let God
be with him, and let him go up unto
Jerusalem. And from the children of
the covenant, the young men gathered to
Jerusalem. The people of the land
rose up to greet them, but one brother fought
another for dominion, and to them
with whom the Lord prevailed, the word of God
was given. And their genealogy
was found therein; yea, even their descent
from Jacob and a knowledge of their right
to be ordained as priests according to
the Order of the Son of God.

And now,
behold, my sons, is not the meaning of
these things as plain as word can be? The Lord,
our Holy King, hath granted your desire
to go unto Jerusalem and seek
out your inheritance, for he hath laid
up treasures not of gold and silver but
of precious ore whose worth shall never dim
with time: my jealous kinsman Laban hath
the sacred record of our people which
Josiah did commission to be kept
on plates of brass. And if ye will attempt,
the Lord will prosper and provide for you
the means whereby ye might obtain these plates,
for he hath given no commandments to
the sons of God save he hath first prepared
a way for them, that they accomplish all
the things which he commandeth them. And are

ye not the children of the covenant? Then rise,
like men; go up unto Jerusalem
once more, and seek the word of God lest we
should lose a knowledge of our fathers and
the goodness of our God, in saving them
from bondage, and our ordinances be
corrupted from their ancient purity.
And come not down again until ye have
obtained the record.

Now, when Lehi made
an end of speaking, Laman marveled that
his father would command him, like a bird
back to its cage, and think that he should sing
for joy to go again unto a land
on which the judgment of Almighty God
must soon descend: its rulers overthrown
and all of its inhabitants enslaved.
And Lemuel did also murmur in
this manner. But when Sam and Nephi heard
the Lord's command, they rent their garments as
a token of their covenant to do
these things and sacrificed a little ewe
lamb, from among the firstlings tended by
their sisters, as a burnt offering.

And
the sons of Lehi traveled to the home
of their rich kinsman in the city, and
they left their father and their mother and
their sisters in a valley by the sea.
And also Olam and his wife remained.
But Olam, being seventy-and-eight
years old, began to be diminished; his
natural force abated, and he died.
And after he was buried, Olam's wife
(and now, behold, her name was Abishag)
rehearsed to Lehi the assurances
made unto Olam: more especially,
that he should be esteemed a brother, not
a servant. Therefore Abishag waxed bold
and asked if Lehi would fulfill the law

himself or if, as proxy, he would give
a son as husband in his stead; for it
had not yet ceased to be with Abishag
after the manner of a woman, and
she still retained her moisture.

And he spake
unto Sariah, saying: Zachiel
saved Hagar in the wilderness and drew
his sword, commanding Sarah to receive
her up again a wife and sister of
an equal stature with herself; but we
have never knelt with Zachiel nor pressed
him for reprieve. What obligation can
we have to one unbound by marriage or
by blood? The law availeth none such.

And
Sariah answered him, What question can
there be of obligation when the law
availeth none, except it turn our souls
to him who veileth our iniquities
and covereth our nakedness in robes
of righteousness and strength? Have ye not called
the law a typifying of his coming? Let
us not, then, hide from its provisions, like
unfaithful servants from their master's gaze,
but ask on what conditions justice, yea,
and mercy also, might be satisfied,
and having chosen, let us seek a sign,
like Gideon, in confirmation of
our resolution.

Lehi said to her,
And what shall be our course? Can justice make
demands upon our bed or ask that we
enlarge our habitation to give place
for strangers? No; though I cut covenants
with Olam, surely I cannot be held
accountable for Olam's covenants
with Abishag. To cast his burdens on
my back would be unjust.

She answered him,
And what of mercy? She hath done no wrong
that she should be left barren and alone,
and we cannot expect the Shepherd to
provide her husband in a thicket when
our sons return to hunt for game. But as
the Suffering Servant hath taken on
himself our griefs and sorrows, surely he
hath given us the law to teach us how
we also ought to bear the burdens of
a neighbor and to love the stranger as
ourselves.

He said unto Sariah, Which
now of your sons and husband, thinkest thou,
should be her neighbor? And whose wife shall she
be made, among the five of us? Perchance
the son ye choose rebuff his bride and it
displease the Lord; would not he slay our son
as he slew Judah's Onan? Tempt them not
with Onan's sins, lest they become a hiss
and byword in the mouths of Israel,
whose daughters speak of onanism with
contempt. And Judah, when he came unto
Tamar, went up in secrecy and shame,
after his wife had died, not knowing her
until she showed the signs and tokens of
his coming unto her. Then how much more
the shame if I should turn aside from thee
whilst thou art living? Far be it from me
to do so unto thee, and let me not
fall into error.

But she answered him,
and said, Transgression giveth no offense
or cause for shame, but sin; on Judah, not
Tamar or Shuah, be the shame. Joined hand
in hand, the wicked shall be punished, but
the seed of them that follow righteousness
shall be delivered. Was not Pharez made
the father of King David? From the same
embrace a crown and condemnation, each

according to their understanding. I
am old and shall not bear again. But stand
ye forth in Olam's stead, and God shall give
thee eden on the lees; as Abishag
was brought to stand before the king and it
was counted unto her for righteousness,
so much the more if thou shalt do it to
the least among us. For myself, I would
that ye remain mine only, but the Lord
hath shewn me linden hills all strewn with leaves,
and though the holy seed be scattered forth,
their substance shall come home unto the stump
like sap returning to its mother roots;
not my will, but the Lord's be done.

And now
Sariah placed a nail, or tent stake, in
her husband's palm, in token of her free
consent that he stretch forth the curtains of
their habitation and enlarge the place
to which their tent gave shade; but she retained
the hammer for herself. And Lehi spake
to Abishag of their decision and
of their intent to seek a sign from God:
how they would lay a fleece upon the ground
at night and pray that it be soaked with dew
though all the earth surrounding it be dry,
and then, again, the second night, how that
the fleece should be left dry though all
around be wet with dew. And Abishag
consented to abide the trial.

And
it came to pass that on the second day,
Sariah rose and left their tent to find
the ground well-watered, but the fleece was dry.
And Lehi, taking Abishag to wife,
fulfilled her week.

And now Sariah, for
the space of fourteen days, had waited for
her sons' returning from Jerusalem;

but on the fifteenth day, she pulled the hair
from off her head and rent her mantle, and
she clothed herself in sackcloth and sat down
among the ashes, weeping bitterly,
like Rachel for her children. And it came
to pass that Lehi counseled patience and
exhorted her to place full trust in him
who sent their sons as agents, to retrieve
the record. But Sariah mourned, and found
no comfort in his admonition, and
reproached him, saying that he was a hard,
unfeeling man who gave no thought for her
security and that her sons were dead
to rise no more because his foolish dreams
and vain imaginings persuaded them
to throw away their lives and perish in
the wilderness. And with this manner of
complaint, Sariah remonstrated with
her husband.

Wherefore, Ruth and Eden gave
her solace, saying, Mother, ye have taught,
and we believe, that God is able to
deliver us from dangers, and the Lord
may yet return to you our brothers; but
if not, we know he will make recompense
and publish peace unto thy soul. Intreat
us not to call thee Mara, for the Lord
shall bless thy latter end, and we shall be
to thee as sons and daughters both, and thou
shalt nurse the sons which we shall bear thee: kings
and priests to rule and reign in Israel
forever. So Sariah girded up
her loins with strength, and she was comforted.

And on that day her sons returned, and she
rejoiced and with her husband offered thanks
for their safekeeping to the Lord. And thus
we see in many cases that the Lord,
who proveth all his children, doth withhold
immediate relief so that we might

FIGURE 10. “The Matriarch Sariah Laments.” Godwin.

be free to choose and not constrained by our
indebted state; and only after we
have passed the trial of our faith do we
perceive the weakness of our faculties,
which cannot comprehend the means whereby
he worketh to effect the immortality
and endless happiness of all mankind
and to deliver us from present fears.

And now it came to pass that Nephi and
his brethren came unto their father's tent
bearing the plates of brass and did relate
the circumstances which attended them
upon their errand for the Lord, and they
did also make excuse for their delay,
explaining how one Zoram, keeper of
the keys for Laban, had been taken up,
to join their company, and waited now
without the camp.

Now these had been their deeds
while they were journeying to get the plates.
Behold, when they had reached the walls about
Jerusalem, they held a council to
determine which among them would go forth
and ask the plates of Laban. And it came
to pass that they cast lots, and Laman thus
was separated from his brethren by
the Spirit of God; or, it seemed to them
that God had given the disposing of
the lot into his lap. But Laban thrust
him out and said he was a robber come
to steal the record of his brethren in
the church and threatened to cut off his hand
if he should come again, pretending that
he was a beggar.

And so Laman and
his brethren traveled to their father's house
and gathered up his gold and silver, and
they came again up to Jerusalem,
desiring Laban that he should accept

their father's treasure on exchange for that
which would preserve their seed from bondage and
from death: a knowledge of the Lord and of
his tender mercies in delivering
their fathers from the Wilderness of Sin—
this notwithstanding their iniquities.
But Laban, not content to trade his brass
for gold, did send his servants forth to slay
the sons of Lehi, and they fled into
the wilderness to hide.

And as they hid,
Laman and Lemuel began to beat
their younger brothers; but there is no place
unknown to God, who sent his messenger
to cry repentance. And the angel said,
Why do ye smite your younger brothers with
a rod? Go up unto Jerusalem
again, as they have counseled, and the Lord
will give the plates into your hands.

And so
they crept in darkness to the city and
did not resolve upon a stratagem
at night-time save it was for Nephi, who
went forth within the walls, and as he made
his way unto the house of Laban, he
beheld the man, there fallen to the earth
before him, drunken. Therefore Nephi took
his sword and slew him, and he dressed himself
in Laban's clothes and breached the safety of
his treasury by speaking with the voice
of Laban unto Zoram, who possessed
the keys, that he should enter in and fetch
the record. And supposing Nephi was
his master, Laban, Zoram gave the plates
into his hands and followed him without
the city walls. But when the other sons
of Lehi rose, he knew that he had been
deceived, and fled, and Nephi gave him chase
and seized him, swearing with an oath that if

he would go down into the wilderness,
he should be free, and travel with them to
a promised land where inequalities
of rank and riches should be done away.
And Zoram swore an oath that he would go
with them to this new land.

Now Lehi had
compassion, when he heard, and sought the place
of Zoram's waiting, in a thicket, where he
verified what had been spoken and
embraced him. And it came to pass that he
rejoiced exceedingly and offered to
the Lord a sacrifice, and he gave thanks
unto the God of Israel for their
return.

But Laman murmured, saying that,
except he had been absent, Abishag
should have been given unto him to wife
and that his father was lascivious.

And Lehi said, Behold, the Lord hath made
it known to me by night that it is an
abomination for a man to seek
out many wives and concubines. The deeds
of David and of Solomon were an
affront to God, for he delighteth in
the chastity of men; wherefore, his face
is turned from those who use the bodies of
his daughters in their lusts, as objects to
be acted on. And now the land of our
inheritance must be preserved from these
iniquities, or we shall be accursed
and our descendants be forsaken of
the Lord. And so a new commandment I
give unto you, that husbands shall have one
wife only; concubines they shall have none.
Howbeit, whatsoever God commands
shall be accounted unto those who do
his will for righteousness, for what is wrong
in certain circumstances may be right

in others, and the Lord desireth that
a righteous branch of Joseph be sent forth
among the olive trees grown wild in his
far-reaching vineyard. Wherefore, he would have
us raise up seed to him, and ye must go
again unto Jerusalem, to call
on Ishmael and ask his daughters to
accept the shade beneath your tents and share
your burdens.

And it came to pass that all
the sons of Lehi hastened to obey
these words, and Zoram also took to wife
the eldest daughter of this Ishmael;
and Lehi's daughters also gave themselves
in marriage to the sons of Ishmael.
And thus they brought forth children: Abishag
bare sons and called her firstborn Jacob, and
the second she called Joseph, saying he
should be the branch to raise an ensign for
the nations spoken of by Lehi. And
they multiplied while in the wilderness,
but not in sorrow, neither did they till
nor sow the ground, but for the space of eight
years traveled in the strength of God, unto
the seashore. And it came to pass that they
grew hale and ate raw meat made sweet, as though
it had been coriander seeds imbued
with honey; and, in the delivery
and nurturing of all their children, strength
was given to the women so that they
could bear with ease the burdens placed upon
their shoulders.

For the Lord directed them
by means of spindles in a ball of brass
which turned and pointed out their path; and it
did work, according to their faith, to guide
them into paths of safety. And that they
might cross those waters to the promised land
and raise up seed unto the Son of Man,

Nephi was shown where he might seek out ore,
to fashion tools wherewith to build a ship,
and also he was shown the pattern for
a ship unlike the vessels made by men.

So they departed from that world unto
a new, and better, taking with them seeds
of every kind and also honey in
abundance. And it came to pass that sharp
contentions did commence between the sons
of Lehi as they crossed the waters, for
Laman and Lemuel made merry, not
observing what was written on the ball
nor calling on the Lord. But they went forth
in their own strength, aroused to action by
zeal without knowledge, lacking charity,
enticed by mead to sing and dance and speak
with rudeness to their parents; wherefore, they
were chastened by their brother, Nephi, who
addressed them with much soberness. And now
it came to pass that they were angry and
did treat him with much harshness, binding him
with cords and smiting him, and saying, We
will not allow our younger brother to
establish personal rule over us.

And after Nephi had been bound, the ball
did cease to work, and they were driven back
before a great and mighty tempest for
the space of three days, swallowed up, almost,
by mountain waves which broke upon them. And
their father, Lehi, chastened them, but they
did threaten him, that they would take his life
if he should speak again for Nephi, that
he might be loosed. Yea, neither would they hear
the pleadings of their wives and children, who
were frightened by the mighty winds which beat
upon them and did plead for the release
of Nephi, who endured his bondage with
longsuffering and praised the name of God
unwearyingly. But their pleas were vain

and fell on stony hearts, for nothing could
persuade Laman and Lemuel to loose
their brother save it were the prospect of
a sudden death and judgment. Wherefore, on
the fourth day, fearing for their lives, they freed
him and restored responsibility
for guiding them across the seas to him
whom God had chosen, notwithstanding his
inferiority of birth, lest they
be shipwrecked and entombed beneath the waves.

And now it came to pass that Nephi prayed
unto the Lord and offered sacrifice,
and he gave thanks for his deliverance
from bondage and petitioned for their safe
arrival in the promised land. Behold,
immediately after he had prayed,
the winds and waves did cease to beat upon
their vessel, and new words appeared upon
the brazen ball, directing Nephi how
to sail their ship to safety.

And it came
to pass that after many days the land
appeared, and they saw naked people and
much water and green trees with many kinds
of fruit. And they went forth and pitched their tents
upon the land, attempting to converse
with its inhabitants according to
their language, but could not interpret what
was spoken; wherefore, Lehi caused that they
should be instructed in his language. And
the people of the land showed Lehi and
his family where ore of iron and
of gold, of silver and of copper could
be found, and Nephi taught his people—for
they truly loved him, and they would that he
should be their king—he taught the ways of God
to all who would believe, and also he
rehearsed to them the goodness of the Lord,
in warning them to flee Jerusalem,

and piloting their feet in paths of truth
and light, and blessing all the labors of
their hands. Now Nephi shared the wisdom he
obtained of God, in artifice of wood
and iron, and of copper and of brass,
of steel and gold and silver; for this cause
a portion of the people loved him and
desired that he should be anointed as
their king. And Lehi spake unto his sons,
Laman and Lemuel, and also to
the sons of Ishmael, and Zoram, and
their seed, exhorting them to hearken to
the voice of Nephi; but they murmured and,
with vain and lying words, persuaded some
among the rising generation that
the heavens had been silenced, after their
arrival in the promised land, and that
their younger brother had no right to make
himself a king.

                                    And now it came to pass
that Lehi went the way of all the earth.

And Nephi's older brothers sought to take
away his life and went forth stirring up
rebellion and pretending he would tax
the people grievously if they should let
him live. And as he lay asleep, the Lord
warned Nephi, in a dream, that he should flee
into the wilderness. And with the moon
to guide his steps, and all who would go with
him, Nephi took his tents and journeyed for
the space of many days, according to
the ball, or compass, which had shown their way
across the sea. And Ruth and Eden, and
his older brother Sam, and Zoram, came
away with him; the sons of Abishag,
his younger brothers, likewise followed him
into the wilderness; and others who
believed the revelations given of
the Lord to Nephi did accompany

them in their flight. And they did call the place
of their retreat the land of Nephi, and
themselves his people. Yea, they took upon
themselves the name of Nephites, and the tribes
which stayed with Laman took upon themselves
the name of Lamanites.

And they were cursed
in this rejection of their brother, like
sinners in the hands of an angry god,
for Nephi took with him the record of
their people and the works of providence
which brought them to the promised land. Behold,
without a knowledge of their history,
they dwindled into unbelief and grew
in wickedness until they had become
a people without principle, beyond
the reach of reason or of feeling.

And
it came to pass that they waged war against
the Nephites, brother fighting brother, and
much blood was shed; but Nephi had prepared
his people to defend themselves against
the Lamanites, and they were prospered by
the Lord. Wherefore, his people multiplied
exceedingly and spread across the land,
becoming rich in gold and silver, and
in precious things. And Nephi, waxing old,
anointed a successor to defend
and labor for his people and bestowed
on him the sword of Laban. And it came
to pass that Nephi died, and hundreds of
his followers had passed away in wars
and bloodshed; wherefore they became a stern
and solemn people. But because of their
great love for Nephi, they did call their kings
in his remembrance: second Nephi, third
Nephi, and so on, stamping each with this
address, according to his reign.

Behold,
for many years the Nephites flourished in
the north and in the south, indulgent laws
securing to the laborer the fruits
of his employment. But contention, in
the days of one Mosiah, stirred the hearts
of all the people up to anger, and
the Lord warned this Mosiah to depart
before the government was overthrown
and all the land of Nephi marched to war.

VI

The conflict of justice twixt Lamanite
and Nephite factions would continue six
hundred years more, but Emma lacked the time
to sit and scribe its end; their daily bread
still needed baking, and the clothes they wore
still needed to be laundered of both dust
and sweat. What peace and quiet she could steal
was tainted by the taste of bile, spued up
in celebration of an answered prayer.
Emma thanked heaven for her pregnancy
but contemplated alterations to
her physiognomy with growing dread—
the swollen stomach; joints so loose it hurt
to swing her legs; a constitution leached
of vital force by some unseen, unknown,
embodied spirit. Haunted by the ghost
of future joys and sorrows, Emma found
it difficult to focus on a past
whose outcome was her present.

She gave up
the pen for good, to Martin Harris, just
as Joseph started in on Abishag
and her experience of childbirth. With
the older man's arrival, Joseph could
proceed apace. He felt no need to stop
the work and finished his dictation of
The Book of Lehi only days before

his bride expected to deliver new
life to the world.

Because sabbatical
succeeds creation, Martin planned a trip
back to Palmyra, asking Joseph leave
to take the manuscript and show his wife
the fruits produced through their financial and
his secretarial support. He asked,
and Joseph asked the Lord, in turn, surprised
to hear the unequivocal response:
a

No

in thunder. To condemn a man
of war, like Samson, for surrendering
to softness is to obfuscate our own
capitulation to the present and
to presence—Martin worried what his wife
would say next week, and Joseph that his most
steadfast adherent would abandon him:
they asked a second time and then a third,
as though they were unable to conceive
another question, or another route
to their desired destination. And thus,
by importunity, they wrested bread
from stones—permission to show Lucy what
her husband offered time and treasure to
deliver into being, with the sole
condition that the manuscript be shown
only to those in Martin's family.

He left, and Alvin came: a tender babe
too like his namesake, he was taken back
to heaven only moments after his
arrival.

Joy aborted, Joseph raged
against divine injustice—how could God
allow the innocent to be removed
involuntarily from loving homes

and sent to hell, for want of water? *His*
the hand that plucks and prunes and his the hand
of judgment—so he thought, but Joseph knew
as little of the Lord, as yet, as trees,
at night, of hydrogen and helium
and nuclear fusion and gravity.
He shed a trail of tears, but night is when
the vapor pressure deficit dips low
enough for trees to grow, and water loss
through transpiration is offset by gains
distilling from the heavens: Emma lived,
and Joseph grew more still, relinquishing
the morrow to itself.

But what became
of Martin? Whence the man? The manuscript
entrusted him? The prophet chased him north,
as though he were a fugitive, but found,
instead, a prodigal. Ashamed, bereft
of that which he had prematurely asked
for, Martin knew that by miscarrying
The Book of Lehi, he had lost his soul
as well as Joseph's only copy of
the transcript.

Joseph learned that he had sinned
as soon as he saw Martin's face and read
therein the news, as though a paperboy
had published Martin's indiscretion—and
his own transgressions—from the housetops. This
first revelation, that a prophet and
a chosen vessel might be torn in two,
emancipated Joseph from the creeds
insisting sin and grace both persevere:
all wrong! Although the God of Heaven gave
him grace sufficient to work miracles,
the war between his vain ambition and
the principles of righteousness was not
concluded, only entering a new
and different phase. If he continued as
he had begun, in faith, and chose the things

that please the Lord, his gift would be restored,
and he might translate once again; but if
he trusted in the flesh and set at naught
the counsels of the Lord, another would
receive an hundred-fold, and he'd be left
with sixty-, thirty-, less—according to
the recompense of God.

That Joseph's first
recorded revelation should condemn
himself—the prophet speaking on behalf
of God—might seem a paradox. But soap
is made on slaughter days: the fat scraped free
of bone and sinew, then repurposed, mixed
with ash and boiled until the lye has lost
its edge—one drop upon the tongue, to test
its alkalinity. Too soon and, like
a coal from off the altar, soap will burn.
Because he burned, the prophet felt himself
forgiven, cleansed of sin, and ready to
continue translating the record.

Still,
he needed an assistant who could take
dictation. Martin had betrayed him;
Emma was yet recovering her strength
after her brush with death; and others he
rejected out of hand, disqualified
through their incontinence or distance from
his home in Pennsylvania. Damned despite
the Lord's forgiveness and unable to
progress until another scribe appeared,
he itched for new intelligence—the thrill
of revelation coursing through his mind,
enlarging his conception of the world
and all that isn't in it. Yes, he itched,
but Joseph kept himself from scratching and,
in stillness, found a new perspective on
the plight of Moses, standing at the shore
and waiting for salvation. Summer flew,
and fall, and winter, fruitlessly, but on

the sixth of April, eighteen twenty-nine,
a blooming bough was grafted on his soul.

Although another year would pass before
the words of Jesus Christ to prophets and
apostles in the Western Hemisphere
were published and his Church established, when
his brother Samuel arrived on foot
in Harmony, delivering a man
called Cowdery for inspection, Joseph sensed
the harvest was at hand. With Oliver
to scribe, The Book of Mormon fairly leapt
from Joseph's lips; the pair sat side-by-side
for hours, the young schoolmaster taking down
dictation from a man who should have been
his pupil. Covered with a linen cloth,
the golden plates lay unconsulted on
their table, like a prop, while Joseph stared
into his seerstone, reading of the church
that Nephi's offspring organized among
the people of the Lord, as Emma worked
and Oliver put pen to paper, each
transfixed by the unfolding story of
a nation fallen from prosperity
to famine, tribalism, and decay—
the narrative disrupted only by
infrequent queries made by Oliver
about the spelling of *Abinadi*
or other matters of transcription.

But
one day in May, as they considered what
he'd written, Oliver asked Joseph when
the Savior would return to earth and give,
again, authority to baptize those
who seek his kingdom; for, without that pearl
of great price, efforts to decode The Book
of Mormon mattered little in the war
between the house of God and Satan's hosts.
Not narrative but power was required
to usher in the peace of Jesus Christ's

millennial administration, so
the prophet recommended that they do
as he had done, when, as a little boy,
he knelt in prayer to ask remission of
his sins and saw the resurrected Man
of Holiness descend in fire which burned
without consuming.

Little thinking that
the son, whose naming by Elizabeth
made men with knives feel insecure, might come
again, or that a woman's chance to be
ordained to priesthood office was at stake,
Emma declined an invitation to
accompany her husband when he left
with Oliver to skirt round furrowed fields,
where buried seeds unfolded to the light,
and scout themselves a sylvan chapel, so
their prayers might be expressed in solitude.
They sought for rights to act—not civilly,
as ministers of law, but in the name
of Father, Son, and Holy Ghost—and both
young men fell back to see their dream made flesh.

In answer to their prayers, a personage
descended, clothed in glory, to declare
the same good news he shared with those who came
to see him in the wilderness and be
immersed in Jordan's current: "I am John,
a fellow servant sent by Peter to
prepare the way for Jesus Christ's return
and to ordain the faithful gathered here
with power." Placing hands on Joseph's head,
he said, "The priesthood held by Aaron, with
the keys of ministering angels and
repentance, for remission of all sin
in those you baptize by immersion, I
confer on you, my fellow servant, in
the name of the Messiah." Then, again,
the son of Zacharias placed his hands

on Oliver, ordaining him a priest
as well.

Withdrawing several paces and
surveying with expectant gaze the beech
and birch and tulip trees surrounding them,
as though he thought a late arrival to
their conference might appear, the angel paused.
How long? Not forty weeks; not twenty-nine
and one half days; not even half an hour,
for fear the seven angels might mistake
his silence as a sign their time had come;
just long enough for Emma, in her home,
to punch the proofing dough back down and set
it farther from the fire, to rise again,
more slowly.

Satisfied, the Baptist spoke
with plainness, giving them instruction as
to how the ordinance of baptism
should be administered, insisting that,
after the sins they had been laden with
were washed away, each lay his hands upon
the other and ordain themselves once more,
this time as members of Christ's body. Then,
the angel promised, Peter, James, and John
would come to seal the oath and covenant
they entered by the Holy Spirit of
the Promise and confer the priesthood named
in honor of Melchizedek, that they
might be endowed with power both to bind
and loose.

So saying, he ascended, and
though Joseph knew no more of when the Lord
would come again, or how the work that he
would do might hasten Christ's return, the weight
of solitary certainty had slipped
from off his shoulders: Oliver had seen
and heard, and in the mouth of two the truth
would be established. With a unity

of purpose, they arose and cut across
the fields towards the Susquehanna and
the Great Physician's remedy for sin,
where Oliver was dipped by Joseph and
the prophet by his scribe.

As each then stood
up dripping, in the stream, the future course
of history was opened to their view:
the trump of Revelation, presaging
combustion and the sacrifice of all
green grass and breathing trees; the second trump,
destroying international accords
and commerce; and the third, foretelling an
unwinding of the social contract by
embittered men who preach impious war.
However, Joseph also understood
the role this priesthood of repentance would
assume in staving off depravity:
the image of his helpmeet's hands appeared,
unbidden, in his mind, depressing rye
and Indian to form a cavity
that held a gill or two of lively yeast;
the upward curving of her lips when she
removed the linen and could see the sponge
had doubled; and the steam exhaled as knife
met crust and wrested life from death, through bread.
He understood, that is to say, how three
measures of meal might come to feed the world
and how the kingdom of Almighty God
would grow from two or three who gathered in
His name until it swept through every clime
and penetrated every continent,
announced in every language and endorsed
in every country, saving not just eight
but eighty billion souls, by—water.

To
the world he made no declaration; to
his wife, who saw his dripping trousers, he
described the Baptist's charge to be made clean

FIGURE 11. "Baptism in the Last Dispensation." Godwin.

of sin, and she entreated him to dip
her in the river also. Joseph gave
his word, but news of Emma's baptism
provoked the skepticism and the scorn
of neighbors who already thought the Hales
had given shelter to a charlatan.
The night before she was to be immersed,
as Isaac Hale glanced out his window, he
caught sight of torchlight and, intuiting
its destination, rushed to meet the band
before they reached his daughter's home. Although
the mobbers had been ready with a rail
for Joseph, none were willing to assault
a man of property and standing, so
negotiation gendered compromise:
the charcoal-painted faces would retreat,
provided Hale could guarantee his son-
in-law would wait to baptize anyone
until he left the county, which they now
expected him to do within the month.
And Emma? Absent as her right to life
eternal was debated, she remained
unbaptized for the nonce, the premium
of Joseph's freedom.

Oliver procured
an invitation from the Whitmers, of
Fayette, New York, with whom the pedagogue
had lived some weeks, like Irving's Ichabod,
as an itinerant instructor to
their fourteen-year-old girl, Elizabeth,
for whom he felt the tug his dowsing rod
once gave him, leaping in his hands, towards
a hidden spring. Her brother David came
to help them move, but only after their
arrival, when Elizabeth explained
the providential circumstances of
his traveling, could Emma, Oliver,
and Joseph understand the Whitmers' faith
that God had brought them to Fayette.

"It was
a miracle," she said, shamefast, "and I
feel highly favored to have witnessed their
leave-taking. David asked, as soon as he
had read your letter, for permission to
depart for Harmony, but Father told
him that he couldn't go until he had
attended to his business here—a field
still needed harrowing, and plaster spread."

"Two days," her brother interjected, "It
was two days' work, at least."

"But when I woke,"
she testified, "the field was white with lime
already for the planting, and I saw
two men retreating through the mist."

"God sent
His angels," David clarified, "to speed
my coming, so that I could help you to
Fayette. We know the work engaging you
has been commissioned by the Father and
are pleased to offer room and board till you
can finish translating the record."

With
renewed intensity, the prophet set
to work among the Whitmers, who took turns
relieving Oliver as scribe. The words
flowed effortlessly from his lips, until
the third time Emma climbed upstairs to ask
when Joseph might be free to drive her in
to town. Delivering a broadside in
response, accusing her of nagging and
impatience, Joseph bowed his head again
to translate and discovered that the words
were gone. He stared into the darkness of
his hat for longer than you might expect
before conceding he would have to ask
forgiveness for his furor if he hoped
to feel, again, the mighty, rushing wind

that shook his limbs like quaking aspen leaves
and set his tongue aflame.

As was his wont,
the prophet sought a quiet stand of trees
in which to pray. Three hours elapsed before
he staggered dripping back, as though a fire
had caused his blood to boil like sap and sent
it steaming out his pores; wrung out and pale
as bone, he stumbled in, clasped Emma's hand,
and begged her pardon. Not with critical
analysis, as if he'd asked for flour
and she stood measuring, but with a free,
unfettered generosity, she gave
it.

"Town ho," Joseph cried and, with renewed
vitality, accompanied his wife
on sundry errands. Locals, who had heard
of heresies and treasure hunting from
the pulpit or the local pump, condemned
them with a glance. But two Canallers, whose
inflexible firmness had scandalized
the gentry, recognized in Joseph's laugh—
as merry as a cricket—something of
their wonted cheer and bowed the couple on
their way. *Good neighbors,* Joseph thought, *though they*
might lack a vine and fig tree, or a wall,
which draws two men of property into
relation, and he drove from Fayette to
the Whitmer farm without another thought
for those who sniggered, as he passed, afraid
of none but God.

Returning to his work,
the prophet spoke again with fluency,
as fast as they could take it down in black
and white, in increments of twenty-five
or thirty words, until the need for food
and drink distracted them. Then tramping down
the stairs to Mother Whitmer's table, they
descended on a spread of sauerkraut

and scrapple; pickled eggs and pretzels; cream
and berries, with abandon. Joseph read,
and his assistants wrote, because no man
can live by bread alone. But what of those
who bake the bread, uncelebrated—no
less serviceable, walking in the path
of duty, than their brethren? Feeling more
like Martha, Mary Whitmer told herself
that women worship silently, and in
support of men ordained to represent
the Lord and speak for him, but pablum of
this sort could not assuage her hunger. *What*
of Deborah, she wondered, *Abigail,*
Priscilla, Phoebe, Junia, Claudia,
and Thecla? The Apostleship might be
reserved for men, but surely I could serve
in some capacity beyond the care
and feeding of voracious boys. In prayer,
she reasoned with the Lord, recounting years
of toil and mourning that the miracle
that lightened David's workload, freeing him
to fetch the Smiths, had also multiplied
her own—more mouths to feed, more bread to bake,
more crumbs which tumbled under table to
be swept. A crumb was all she asked: not for
relief from labor but a glimpse, a taste
of what she labored for; one morsel of
the manna gathered word by word, above
her head, as she stood measuring out flour.

Persuaded or portuned—whatever His
pure purpose—God responded to her prayer
in mercy. While her family and guests
still lay abed the morrow morning, Mary drudged
inside the cowshed, gently wiping down
each teat before massaging it from top
to bottom, crooning in a quiet voice,

> *"So sind wohl manche Sachen,*
> *Die wir getrost belachen,*
> *Weil unsre Augen sie nicht sehn."*

FIGURE 12. "A Witness for Mary Whitmer." Godwin.

A brimming pail in either hand, she picked
her way across the yard, arrested by
the advent of an unfamiliar face,
which blinked into existence as she walked—
a face attached, she noticed, glancing down,
to arms and hands, which held a bundle of
some weight. That strength belied the whiteness of
his beard, suggesting a maturity
attained through strenuous experience
beyond the cloister's walls. Before he spoke
she had already guessed his purpose and
identity, so setting down the milk,
she waited patiently, to see and hear
about his burden.

Not a dream, this face-
to-face encounter with an angel, who
behaved as though he were a neighbor, come
to call on her. "Good morning, Mary," he
began, and transferring his satchel to
the ground, reached out a hand in greeting. She
received it in her own and recognized
the tokens of a fellow laborer—
the callused palm and hardened fingers of
a working man. As Thomas had, she, too,
could handle him and see the signs of his
reality: a shadow stretching past
her feet, across the timothy; a fleck
of spit dried white between his lips; a small
repair to his neat homespun suit. Not much,
in fact, to show he was an angel, but
the matron was untroubled by his plain
attire and speech.

"Good morning," she replied,
"and how might you be called?"

"Moroni is
my name, and I've been sent from God, that you
might know that the interpretation of
this record has been given by the hand
of Jesus." Reaching in his knapsack, he

withdrew the golden plates and held them up
for her inspection, giving an account
of their creation and the part he played
in guiding Joseph to their resting place.
And in conclusion, he declared, "If there
are faults, they are errata introduced
by men; condemn it not because of the
conducing means that God makes use of, for
it is the most correct of any book
on earth, and all who heed its precepts will
be privileged to become acquainted with
the Holy One, who sells to her that hath
no money and reveals himself to her
that hath no standing to demand it." With
these final words he vanished, leaving her
to ponder the impossible.

Among
the peoples of the earth, her name has been
forgotten. Martin, Oliver, and her
son David sought the honor for themselves
and testified to all the world that they
had heard the voice of God declare The Book
of Mormon to be true; that they had seen
Moroni come from heaven clothed in light
and glory, carrying the golden plates
for their inspection. These Three Witnesses,
and Eight to whom the prophet showed the plates
himself, permitting them to heft and see
and handle, gave their signatures as proof
of sensory experience with God
and gold, endorsing Joseph's claims, and they
live on in every copy of the book,
while she—the first and only witness whom
the Lord selected—fades from memory,
just one more Mary overshadowed by
eleven men.

But what was Joseph Smith's
alternative, when women in New York
were legal chattels and a century
would pass before the state admitted them

in jury boxes? Statutes there required
that *three to nine male persons should transact*
affairs concerning the creation of
a new religious corporation, so
of course the five that Joseph culled, from more
than fifty gathered at the Whitmer home
on April sixth, were men. A year had passed
since Oliver's arrival, but the book
was published and a church established; time
enough, at that pace, for the prophet to
address misogyny and any form
of prejudice forestalling Zion in
the years to come. Or so, at least, he might
have thought, if he had seen the problems in
relying wholly on the sterner sex
to promulgate Christ's mercy and preside
over his plan of happiness.

His main
concern, in eighteen thirty, was escape—
from persecution, prosecution, and
the prostitution of his message. Word-
for-word, but out of context, lawyers framed
his declaration of the gospel truth
as an incitement to disorderly
behavior, and although they lost before
the judges, Joseph's enemies prevailed
in courts of public sentiment. A mob
was raised and extralegal violence planned,
but Oliver and Joseph heard of their
intent and fled the scene, a heartbeat in
advance of their pursuers, to the woods
near Joseph Knight's estates in Colesville. No
wagon that night, to speed their journey; its
destruction had appeased the lawless last
time Joseph visited the Knights, and so
they raced on foot through mud and mire until
the schoolmaster collapsed.

The prophet, who
remembered running on another night,
with fifty pounds of gold to weigh him down

and no companion, bent to lift him up
and whisper words of cheer, but Oliver
threw off his arm and cried, in pique, "How long?
O, God! How long have we to be pursued
until you let us rest?" Then, *deus ex*
machina, light—three angels introduced
themselves, descending with the dawn to share
their apostolic power: Peter, James,
and John.

Their faces streaked with dust and sweat,
the fugitives knelt dumbly mute before
the fishermen, uncomprehending. Who
can say why God sends angels after his
anointed have been forced to flee, and not
preveniently? Ask Elijah, who
ran forty days and nights from Jezebel's
assassins with the strength imparted by
God's messenger—but only after he'd
exhausted his own powers and laid down
to die. No explanation for the time
and place of ordination was proposed;
no words of protest offered. Each received
the laying on of hands and was sent off
by men who faded on the crowing of
a cock.

Sent off, but where? The men who'd chased
them seemed to have disbanded with the dawn,
yet Joseph knew the night's unrest would be
recurrent if he lingered in New York,
and Pennsylvania's welcome promised to
be just as rude; the neighbors Isaac Hale
negotiated with expected him
to keep his distance. Harmony would turn
to discord in a trice if he returned.
The answer—inconceivable to one
who'd never heard of Kirtland; couldn't guess
who Sidney Rigdon was; and didn't know
his funeral would antecede the Saints'
arrival at a final resting place—
escaped him. So, until the time was ripe,

he paced the stone, deferring his desire
for destination and responding to
the exigencies of each moment with
an open-ended interest, waiting for
the Lord of Harvests to reveal his will.

Between appearances in court, he hid
with family and friends, until he'd run
iteratively through them all. The fixed
foot of a compass, Joseph jostled back
and forth in search of stillness, wearing through
the fragile fabric of society—
unmoving only by comparison
with his companion, roaming from
Ohio to the Mississippi and
the western borders of Missouri on
a mission to the Indians.
But Oliver's evangelism met
with more success among the Baptists led
by Rigdon than in Shawnee council tents,
so Joseph pivoted. In processing
the news that hundreds had been baptized and
that members of the church in Kirtland now
outnumbered those familiar with his face,
who'd knelt with him in prayer and listened to
him testify of visions, golden plates,
and angels, he discerned the voice of God
and called a scribe to take dictation:

"Thus
have I, the Lord your God, commanded: that
my church shall go to the Ohio and
assemble there against the enemies
conspiring to destroy my doctrine. And
again, I say that ye shall not go up
from thence until the gospel has been preached
in regions round about, for I have much
people who pray to me in faith, and they
must also hear my word. And they shall be
a strength to bolster thee, as Aaron was
to Moses. Here is wisdom, but behold,
let every man and woman choose, for they

are agents to themselves until I come.
Amen."

No hesitation on the part
of Emma, who declared herself prepared
to go without a backward glance, despite
her delicate condition, so with hand
in hand, they left New York to seek a place
of rest. The residue came after, at
a measured pace, disposing of their homes
and land to seek the mansions promised by
their Savior, like a walk of snails that shed
its shells in search of something better: a
cocoon, perhaps, a tomb from which they might
emerge kaleidoscopically—with wings.
They bade farewell to friends and willingly
accepted a surcease of neighborly
associations as the foreseen price
of metamorphosis.

But others paid
unwillingly. The twins that Emma bore
in Kirtland joined her firstborn, in a shroud,
and Joseph might have lost himself again,
in rage, if overreaching death had not
provided consolation. Not content
to swallow up Louisa, Thaddeus,
and Alvin Smith, the greedy grave laid claim
to Emma's counterpart: a mother named
Julia Murdock, who gave birth—a mile
away, the very day that Joseph held
his children for the first and final time—
to twins who lived. Their father, John, gave up
the pair to Emma's care, considering
himself ill-suited to the labor of
dry-nursing two small babies.

"Children are
entitled to be reared by father and
by mother both," he said, depositing
the infants in her arms, then turning to
embrace the prophet, "and the Lord made known

to me that though you are not yet as Job,
in all that you have suffered to defend
the name of Jesus Christ, your recompense
will be the same. And as an earnest of
that promise, I entrust you with my son
and daughter, to instruct and raise as though
they had been born to you, possessing and
receiving every right to their respect
and filial affections prior to
the morning of the resurrection, when
your own sweet babes will be restored to you
again."

Providing for the physical
necessities of newborns, Emma and
the prophet found themselves exhausted at
the end of every evening and collapsed
together on their corn shuck mattress for
a first sleep. After caring for the twins,
whose mewling cries awoke them in the dark,
young lovers made the most of their dorveille
before returning to the angle of
repose, in right relation to the world
and one another, for a second sleep.
But their biphasic slumber seemed to leave
the couple more fatigued each morning than
they'd been at night, and Joseph joked about
how much he missed his moonlight races through
the woods: "At least on those occasions I
could wrestle my pursuer, if he caught
me, for my freedom; now, a wrestle might
increase the number of those keeping me
awake. Like Hercules, I find that two
new heads are born whenever mine is laid
to rest, and rectifying this affair
will be my greatest labor." Jesting words,
but Joseph knew himself oracular
in their pronouncement—that the Lord would find
his efforts to restore the primitive
perfection of his gospel wanting, if
he overlooked weightier matters of

the law, including those whose weariness
found refuge at his breast. So Joseph paced
their little cabin floor and comforted
the children in his arms with lullabies,
in answer to the questions they had not
yet learned to ask.

The questions he himself
most wanted answered—How could he discern
authentic portents of the Spirit from
deceitful workings of the devil? Where
would all his followers arriving from
New York find lodging? When would he be told
to build the city Zion? Which of all
the Indians would be his allies in
that project? What would Emma say if he
brought home a chief for dinner?—they could wait
until his family was settled. Here
he saw a future worth the struggle they'd
endured: no mobs to mar the evening calm;
no plates of gold or irreplaceable
translation to protect; and no new tears
to cry above an empty crib. Until
a servant could be found, the twins would need
their undivided interest, Joseph knew,
but Emma had already spoken with
the Alger girl and thought her willing, if
Clarissa would consent. The church could wait
a month or two, while he and Emma caught
their breath and let domestic joys possess
them. Joseph, now that he had been ensconced
in Kirtland's safety and society,
surrounded by his followers and friends,
might rest at last, with confidence he'd yet
accomplish all that God could ask of him
in building up The Church of Jesus Christ.

ACKNOWLEDGMENTS

If there is anything virtuous, lovely, or of good report in these pages, John Talbot deserves a good share of the credit. Without his encouragement and example, this book likely would not exist; until he invited me—and other undergraduates studying "Classics and the English Tradition" under his tutelage—to demonstrate my understanding of the epic form by composing one hundred lines of my own, I had yet to commit any of my ideas about Joseph Smith to paper. Those initial lines were terrible, and John, who is one of the best poets of his generation, did me the great service of saying so. But stubbornness and hubris drove me on in one revision after another, and I hope this final product is a more felicitous representation of all I learned from him than that first, wretched draft.

Other teachers played pivotal roles in shaping my understanding of Dante, Milton, and Melville, among others, including Madison Sowell, Neal Kramer, John Tanner, Reid Barbour, Timothy Marr, Steve Walker, Matthew Wickman, and Eliza Richards. I owe them professional and personal debts that cannot be discharged in this limited space. Of course, none of these generous mentors even knew that I was writing *Joseph*, much less that I left their offices dreaming of a creative application for the critical approaches they urged me to consider.

The friends in whom I did confide were gracious enough not to laugh at me. Cassie Peach and Maura D'Amore and Meredith Farmer and Edward Whitley and LuElla D'Amico reassured me that it was safe to disclose my identity as an epic poet. John McWilliams, who I never had the pleasure of meeting, and Christopher Phillips, who is a beloved colleague, wrote books on the American epic tradition that shaped my thinking about what it might mean to forge Joseph's story within the confines of this particular genre.

Two early readers provided encouragement without which I might have abandoned the epic entirely. I will forever be grateful to the late Clayton Christensen. In 2007, he made the time to read an early draft and provided feedback nurturing my belief in the poem's future. And some years later, Kylan Rice, who is a far more gifted writer than I, persuaded me to pluck my epic off the shelf and return to it with a seriousness of purpose. The best of friends, he volunteered to read it in draft form several times and persuaded me to think more about each line as a discrete unit.

When it came time to finish and pitch the manuscript, I was encouraged by Zachary Davis and Justin Collings, talented writers whose epics I hope to see bound on my shelves, alongside this book. Alison Syring took a chance on *Joseph* even though the University of Illinois Press hasn't traditionally published much in the way of creative writing. Without her advocacy, this manuscript might never have seen the light of day. Christopher Jones and the other advance readers she identified provided fantastic feedback and kind appraisals that spurred the project along. Others at the Press have been similarly wonderful to work with: Leigh Ann Cowan, Jennie Fisher, Renee Cote, Charrice Jones, Jennifer Argo, Jim Proefrock, and Jason Gabbert. Jason's cover for the book is so good that I have wondered whether my words can possibly live up to the expectations of greatness his cover cultivates. Of course, Jason's work features the fabulous illustrations of Godwin, who has been an amazing creative partner: visionary, responsive, generous, and professional. I'm so grateful to see my words come to life through his art and hope to work with him again in the future.

My collaboration with Godwin was made possible, in part, by institutional support. Colleagues at Colorado State University, especially Dan Beachy-Quick and Lillian Nugent, have cheerily endorsed this quirky turn in my career, and provided a professional home that made this project possible. I am so thankful for them and for my students at CSU and Brigham Young University, who have marched through many an epic with me over the past fifteen years.

Members of my extended family listened patiently, over an even longer period, to what was likely a tiresome series of updates about this project; they have been my first and best supporters. Richard, my oldest brother, began writing poems long before I was born, and I grew up reading his verses with aspirational wonder. My nephew, Tanner Schenewark, has been a fantastic cheerleader and swapped stanzas with me more than once. Gabriel, my oldest son, grew into his own as a writer just in time to be an interesting conversation partner, challenging my thinking about the poem's aims and structure. Each of his siblings has proudly described me to friends or strangers as a poet, providing me with ample motivation to prove them honest.

For many years, Alana saw every line before anyone else, and she believed that the poem would eventually be published even when I did not. I love her and have thought about how she would respond to a given word or line throughout the writing process. She is not a muse, but a help meet for my best, celestial self, who delivered me from depression and cultivated my highest, holiest aspirations.

Only my father Kenneth believed in *Joseph* more fervently than she did. For more than a decade, whenever we spoke on the phone, he asked me how the poem was coming. As I finished each new section, he asked to read it, then wrote back with a list of questions and suggestions. He loved to write poetry himself, and although Rich was the more immediate influence, he is the fountainhead from which our familial love of the written word flows. Even after his death in 2021, I have felt myself motivated both by his memory and his presence. I love him and can't wait for our next chance to talk poetry.

ZACHARY MCLEOD HUTCHINS is a professor of English at Colorado State University. He is the author of *Before Equiano: A Prehistory of the North American Slave Narrative* and *Inventing Eden: Primitivism, Millennialism, and the Making of New England,* as well as two devotional books written for Latter-day Saint readers—*The Best Gifts: Seeking Earnestly for Spiritual Power* and *Shall I Have Pleasure? An Answer for Sarah.*

The University of Illinois Press
is a founding member of the
Association of University Presses.

Composed in 10.5/13 Mercury Text
with Trajan Pro display
by Jim Proefrock
at the University of Illinois Press
Manufactured by Sheridan Books, Inc.

University of Illinois Press
1325 South Oak Street
Champaign, IL 61820-6903
www.press.uillinois.edu